Praise f

"Janet & I were 2 of the biggest dreamers on the planet . . . she as a gymnast and me as a hopeful NFL player. We realized as we chased our dreams that there was a price to be paid and obstacles to be overcome. There are the doubters, the competition, rules & regs, fatigue, fear, and risks . . . all to be managed and conquered.

However, the one enemy that tears away at your inner psyche is stress. It can control your mood, your body, your appetite, sleep, confidence . . . and ruin relationships and kill dreams. People are often afraid or ashamed of admitting that they are stressed and are unwilling to deal with it. They would have a coach for training, skills & diet but not for one of the biggest hurdles to be cleared to reach their full potential . . . stress!

Drs. Cathy Greenberg & Relly Nadler are an invincible team and together they give us the game plan to reduce the stress & fear that turns our dreams into nightmares. It is never too late to get into the game . . . so get off the bench and take control of your goals & visions and team up with Cathy & Relly to live a stress less, fear less life! *WIN THE DAY!*"

—Vince Papale, featured in "Invincible",
staring Mark Wahlberg

"Emotional Brilliance is an excellent read centering on the practical aspects of leadership, success and failure. The strength of relating the advice and stories from such a diverse group of leaders cannot be understated. This should be required reading especially for young aspiring leaders who will benefit immensely from the many exercises and techniques detailed in the book. There are many books on leaders, but only a handful that strips away theoretical and focuses on what you need to know and put into practice to be a successful leader."

—Ed Hanko, VP Global Security Aramark,
Former FBI SAC, Special Agent in Charge & Operational
Support Section Criminal Investigations.

"Today's business leaders must fight to win the renewed support of a skeptical public—not through new products, fads, or other manipulations—but with the foundations of ethical absolutes that are demonstrated in their reasoning and the decisions that follow. Emotional Brilliance can be your secret weapon to leading with unyielding integrity. Greenberg and

Nadler remind us that we need to take the first step toward producing better business leaders by changing our own ideas about what behaviors are essential to "win".

—Noel Tichy, Professor, University of Michigan,
and author of Succession: Mastering the
Make-Or-Break Process of Leadership Transition

"Based on my experience in pioneering the field of "emotional intelligence" from the early 1980s, I see a clear progression from (1) defining to (2) measuring and, eventually, (3) applying this important concept. The prime purpose of this journey has been to create a human evolution in behavior, which aims at better understanding ourselves and others in order to live a more productive, constructive and fulfilling life. Drs. Greenberg and Nadler's *Emotional Brilliance* represents a key element in this critical evolutionary step. Their contribution to this journey is not only designed to help us cope more effectively with daily demands and pressures, but to thrive! They positioned NAME as their approach to achieving this, with an array of straightforward and practical approaches that provides the reader with numerous tips and hands-on suggestions on how best to do this."

—Reuven Bar-On, PhD,
Executive Director of Bar-On Test Developers,
Author of the Bar-On Emotional Quotient Inventory (EQ-i), Author of
the Bar-On Multifactor Measure of Performance (MMP)

"The mission of "Emotional Brilliance" closely matches ours at NewDay USA; to provide a short cut to greater freedom with easy tools and language to identify and conquer fear, frustration and the daily anxiety of an uncertain world. We both provide a way to be your best in the moment—It's an investment in ourselves."

—Rear Admiral Thomas Lynch, USN (ret),
Chairman, NewDay USA

"We're excited to share proven tips and tools from "Emotional Brilliance" with our community of over 100,000 leaders at the Growth Institute, to hyper-boost any teams bounce back strategy by managing the critical element of emotional chaos to achieve your best year possible."

—Verne Harnish, Author of Scaling Up
and Daniel Marcos, Co-Founders of Growth Institute

"Toughness requires strength. Strength requires vulnerability.

As a former World MMA Champion who holds the UFC record for most wins and minutes fought in the heavyweight division, I have to process my emotions in the moment. Controlling reactions inside the cage, focuses everything I have on my opponent. *Emotional Brilliance* can help you win in the game of life."

—Andrei Arlovski, UFC,
MMA Heavyweight World Champion

"Don't hide your emotions; Greenberg and Nadler share how to use your emotions to leverage success. *Emotional Brilliance* gives the tools, stories, and inspiration to use your emotions, including fear and anger, to enhance creativity, strengthen relationships, and achieve the goals you thought were out of reach."

—Marcia Reynolds, PsyD, MCC, past ICF President,
and author of Coach the Person,
Not the Problem and Outsmart Your Brain

"Greenberg and Nadler are two emotional intelligence and executive coach experts whose new work, *Emotional Brilliance*, teaches us a new, easy to use, clever roadmap for harnessing the power of our feelings for extraordinary results. This is an incredibly valuable volume for coaches, leaders and parents."

—Jeffrey E. Auerbach, Ph.D., MCC; President,
College of Executive Coaching,
and co-author of Positive Psychology in Coaching

"Drs. Greenberg and Nadler offer a fresh approach to understanding and working with emotional intelligence (EI). Straightforward, easy to understand, and tools are included so that the reader can quickly understand their "go to" emotions and better choose how to more effectively manage emotional reactions to just about anything. *Emotional Brilliance* brings new clarity to understanding and building EI skills."

—Ed Nottingham, Ph.D., PCC,
Consulting & Clinical Psychologist,
Author of It's Not as Bad as It Seems:
A Thinking Straight Approach to Happiness

"*Emotional Brilliance* builds upon the ever-crucial concept of emotional intelligence, guiding us to recognize and delineate our emotions and then manage them in a healthy and beneficial style. A common question of the EI specialist is "what next?" By focusing on the "doing" more than the "thinking," *Emotional Brilliance* fills that void, providing a pathway to being an elite practitioner of emotional intelligence. The chosen path is up to us!"

—Captain Don Kester, (ret) SWAT & Crisis Management

"Emotional leadership is easy when things are going well. During times of crises and uncertainty, effective emotional leaders separate their organizations from the rest of the pack. EMOTIONAL BRILLIANCE provides critical insight on how to keep your organization on the leading edge."

—Paul J. Menzel, CEO Financial Pacific Leasing

"Nadler and Greenberg warmheartedly deliver the essence of emotional intelligence in their models and tools to enhance performance at work and beyond. In our uncertain and evolving world, 'Emotional Brilliance' can help you lead a more stress resilient, calm and fearless life reimagining what's possible cultivating a kinder and more compassionate world that nourishes and serves all human beings."

—Dr. Maynard Brusman, Consulting Psychologist & EQ Leadership Executive Coach

"When a human challenges the body's capability during mega-ultramarathons, there is a formula that can be quantitatively calculated. Fueling strategies equate to X, Training plans Equate to Y, Effective Gear equates to Z, and the result is then subject to the number of participants, but these are all standard tools that any athlete can acquire with intermediate level commitment. A pure athlete is an explorer; the person who can reach into their deepest fears and turn that fear into fuel and that fuel is mental and emotional tenacity."

—Christopher Guerra, Forged Glory Athletics, Founder/Coach/Athlete, Patience-Presence-Positivity

EMOTIONAL BRILLIANCE™

EMOTIONAL BRILLIANCE™

LIVING A STRESS LESS, FEAR LESS LIFE

CATHY L. GREENBERG, PHD
RELLY NADLER, PSY.D

Waterside Productions

Copyright © 2020 by Cathy L. Greenberg and Relly Nadler
www.eblifebook.com

Emotional Brilliance™ and EB™ are registered trademarks
NAME™ is a registered trademark
All rights reserved. This book or any portion thereof may not be reproduced or used in any manner whatsoever without the express written permission of the publisher except for the use of brief quotations in articles and book reviews.

Printed in the United States of America

First Printing, 2020

ISBN-13: 978-1-949001-36-5 print edition
ISBN-13: 978-1-949001-37-2 eBook edition

Waterside Productions
2055 Oxford Ave
Cardiff, CA 92007
www.waterside.com

EMOTIONAL BRILLIANCE™

Access Bonus Tools, Tips & Resources
Valued at over $299
You need to enhance Your Emotional Brilliance™

http://eblifebook.com

*Your gift for rising above success to significance
from the authors
Dr. Cathy and Dr. Relly*

TAKE ACTION!

To our future together

CATHY'S DEDICATION
To Olivia Paige and all the little ones in our clan who will read this one day and understand their Go To is more than Nutella.

To my mother Barbara and her two sisters, Carol and Nancy, rearranging heaven with my grandmother Ella. Her Go To was "Darlin, relax, before ya'll have a spell or something."

To my father, Bernie (a.k.a. Bob London) who taught me my Go To "Adapt or be disappointed" and who lived by his "Show an act of unexpected kindness every day."

RELLY'S DEDICATION
To my father Martin, his Go To: "They can't make it tough enough for me."

To my mother Ann who exuded love and positive regard.

To my sister Nancy whose Go To was gratitude and all things nature.

"You can act to change and control your life; and the procedure, the process, is its own reward."

—A<small>MELIA</small> E<small>ARHART</small>

CONTENTS

Foreword by Marshall Goldsmith   *xiii*
Introduction by Obed D. Louissaint   *xvii*
Preface   *xix*

CHAPTER ONE   1
Your Emotional Ecosystem

CHAPTER TWO   31
Truths and Illusions

CHAPTER THREE   41
Evolution of Emotions: Research Made Easy

CHAPTER FOUR   63
Big Picture, Big Results

CHAPTER FIVE   71
Your Emotional Brilliance: Take Action

CONCLUSION   115

Case Studies   *119*
NAME™ Template   *123*
Bibliography   *135*
Acknowledgments   *139*

FOREWORD

Welcome to the "new normal" . . . again! Oh, and by the way, what do those words really mean for you this time, or for any of us for that matter? Something to think about isn't it; at least for those of us who have come to realize that our world is meant to evolve, and as it does, so do we. Or do we?

We never imagined before 9/11 that we'd traipse in our socks, or worse, our bare feet, into enhanced screenings by a newly expanded law enforcement group called the TSA. But we've adapted to following TSA regulations because we're on the road more often than not and we just want it to go smoothly. Still, we have learned to anticipate a rise in blood pressure standing in line with the bi-annual vacation traveler. The one in front, the fumbler having a loud and dramatic conversation on their cell while loading their security bin as we all strain to keep our cool by looking at our smart gadget, concurrently checking the time for our flight's departure.

Here's another thought: if we choose not to follow the "new normal," what happens? And more importantly, if we take this journey to a place called the "new normal" with all our brother and sister earthlings, will they act accordingly?

Just reading these words can trigger anxiety, sadness, overwhelm or exhaustion. When did anything "new" other than expecting a child or planning that dream vacation feel great?

In Doctors Greenberg and Nadler's evolved dictionary of emotional intelligence, it depends on our Emotional Brilliance™. EB™ is a process beyond simply managing ourselves or managing our emotional selves with others.

EB™ is a no-fail way for us to find our "Go To" emotions and feelings that become our unique sweet spot to master and leverage that untimely moment we cannot predict—anytime, anywhere—through the use of a simple model called NAME™; an easy way to Notice, Accept, Manage, and Express our feelings most appropriately.

More simply, if a map is our array of emotional intelligence traits, your address is your Emotional Brilliance™; if your wardrobe is your array of emotional intelligence traits, your khaki slacks and green shirt are your Emotional Brilliance. You know where you live so you know you can always get there. You know what clothes look best on you so you know you can always figure out what to wear. See the pattern? You know where to find what you need just when you need it. Emotional Brilliance™ is the way to find your best emotional self when you need it, especially on the road to your "new normal." By using the tips in this book, you can count on it showing up and being available when you need it. All you need to do is look for it, keep it close, and help it flourish.

Cathy Greenberg and I have been friends and colleagues for more than twenty-five years. We've been great fans of each other's work since the beginning because we both value living what we write about. Cathy has been dealt a hand with which she could have easily crumbled. Instead, she has turned difficulties into success. And you'll learn more about her on her own road to Emotional Brilliance™, as well as about Relly's.

Having learned about their deep expertise and life's work on emotional intelligence, I can see how Cathy and Relly have teamed up to present one of the easiest to remember yet powerful techniques for dealing with defining moments before they define you. With exercises and practical hands-on tips, *Emotional Brilliance: Living a Stress Less, Fear Less Life* will give you everything you need to overcome your emotional bad habits, and learn to create "healthy emotional hygiene," as the Dali Lama likes to say. After all, emotions are contagious; in fact, they can be more lethal than a virus. Reading *Emotional Brilliance*™ will help you embrace and come to grips with your emotional baggage so the next time travel takes you through a TSA screening with that traveler fumbling on their phone, you'll be more "inoculated" with EB™ and less "infected" by inconsiderate behavior, leaving you with more Emotional Brilliance™ for the remainder of your journey to success, wherever that may lead.

Marshall Goldsmith
La Jolla, California

MARSHALL GOLDSMITH is a *New York Times* bestselling author or editor of more than thirty-four books, and Thinkers50 Hall of Fame inductee.

INTRODUCTION

The world has fundamentally changed, and that was even before the global pandemic. But now, the change is being accelerated at a pace we've not seen before. As individuals, we must find new ways to create value and become indispensable to our employers. How? Curiosity, combined with an insatiable appetite for learning, is imperative to succeed in today's workplace, and has become increasingly important. And yet, there's still so much to learn.

One of the biggest accelerators of change today is technology. I am convinced that 100 percent of jobs will be impacted by artificial intelligence and automation, with the movement already underway begun. As the months and years progress, we will see the rate of change increase dramatically. The reality is that as tasks are redistributed between people and machines, the value of skills that people have increases, with everyone becoming more experienced and productive with better tools. It's about human + machines vs. machines only.

I often think of this transition to be like that in the Industrial Revolution, when the horse and carriage was being rapidly replaced by the modern technology of that time—the automobile. Carriage drivers had to learn to drive an automobile and get hired to operate something completely new, replacing what they were familiar with their entire lives. The job or the profession fundamentally changed, but the problem they were seeking to solve—transporting passengers from one place to another—persisted over time. Their opportunity, much like ours today, leans into the technological revolution and importance of a modernized skill set.

While all jobs will be impacted, I think very few will be eliminated entirely. As a matter of fact, many new jobs will be created, and I see a net gain in employment opportunities. It will require the organization and individual to invest in the necessary re-skilling and up-skilling to adapt to these changes.

Skills are the key to managing the transition and creating value to make ourselves indispensable. Do you excel at accounting, computer programming, or sales? Those hard skills are the ones most in flux. But soft skills like learning agility, growth mindset, curiosity, self-awareness, and relationship building all have stability and continuity. These soft skills, which require creativity and critical thinking from people, transcend the acceleration of change and will always remain vital to a business throughout any kind of technological revolution. Naturally, growth is necessary, but being a good listener and demonstrating empathy will never become outdated or outsourced.

We also speak of employment training in terms of skilling, re-skilling, and up-skilling. What has become increasingly apparent is this same need for adaptability outside the workplace, and the importance to apply these same principles to each person's emotional adaptability as well. This is where *Emotional Brilliance* comes in.

This book provides an effective approach to not only help your professional career, but your personal growth as well. As is so often the case nowadays, what happens on the job affects relationships at home. Doctors Greenberg and Nadler bring to light this merging of what used to be separate lives, now coexisting under one roof, and offer a single formula that can be applied consistently between both worlds. The tools provided in their book work equally as well in the office and at home.

During these trying times, when we are all reeling from information overload, the plan laid out in *Emotional Brilliance* gives straightforward, no-nonsense steps to help us remain fearless and keep our strong place in the world, while at the same time, live stress free and be fulfilled in our lives at home with the ones we care about the most.

Obed D. Louissaint
VP, Talent, IBM Global

PREFACE

For good emotional health, we need to learn to manage emotions in ourselves, and to some degree in others, or at least how we respond to others. This requires an emotional immune system. Just as we learned to adapt and heal after 9/11, we will do the same now in response to the 2020 global pandemic by rising to the physical, mental, and financial challenges, and the associated set of emotional ones like anxiety, suspicion, regret, sorrow, scarcity, and helplessness.

The result will be a constructive environment within yourself—an emotional ecosystem built on your calm mind and soothing emotions—from which you can see and express yourself more clearly and realistically. Emotional Brilliance™ is an essential part of creating and maintaining your healthy internal environment as well as being essential to your external success in your professional and personal life.

This book is a field guide to help you quickly establish habits for your emotional hygiene based on four steps: (1) Notice and Name, (2) Accept, (3) Manage, and (4) Express in what we call the NAME™ process.

CHAPTER ONE

"Your future depends on many things, but mostly on you."
—Frank Tyger

Marcus "Conan" Silveira, professional athlete, Extreme Fighting champion, Ultimate Fighting Championship (UFC) Coach of American Top Team

A lot of people used to think that putting two guys in a steel cage to fight it out was a death wish. Not me. When I started at age fourteen, I was extremely happy. I loved fighting. Even saying I loved fighting is only half-way true. The same with saying it was my passion. Because I believed and still believe it is what I was put on this earth to do. Back then, it was anything goes. No real rules except for maybe two: no eye gouging, and no fish-hooking, which is when you stick a few fingers in a guy's mouth and drag him by his cheek. Back then, they said there was something wrong with us. Then it grew into what was called Extreme Fighting, and they said we were street thugs. Today, it's a big business known as mixed martial arts, MMA, the fastest growing sport in the world, and now they say we're exciting entertainment. Bleacher Report says, "Fans can relate on a deep emotional and empathetic level."

Maybe they're right about our fans, except for the ones who just get off on seeing us beat the crap out of each other. As a coach now to championship MMA fighters and those with the goal to become champions, I tell every one of them fighting is full of emotions. I say to them, "You're always going to have them. So my question to you is how many fights do you need to have under your belt before you can say 'I'm in control of everything. Five hundred fights and I'm not going to feel nervous anymore. I'm not going to have my guts go up and down anymore. My mind isn't going to explode with so many questions anymore: Did I train right? Did I sleep right? Did I kick right? Did I go to the mat right? Is he right? Is she right?'"

Most matches are won or lost before an MMA fighter even steps into the cage. Being mentally tough is part of it. But you have to be emotionally tough, too. Back in the days leading up to a match, or even at the moment I stepped into the cage, I didn't feel nervous. Not that I'm special, I just had a different way, or a better way, of dealing with emotions. "Oh, I don't feel anything." B.S., of course I do. I'm alive. I have blood in my veins. I'm always going to feel something. What makes the difference is how I choose to feel or deal with something. So before the fight, in the fight, and after the fight, it was a pleasure. I felt good about it.

What I tell my fighters is they're part of a bigger moment. A part of a moment that is already there and they walk inside that moment. What this means is you never want to try to change it, but what you can change is how you face the moment, how you deal with the moment. Because that is your option.

What I tell them is as the days get closer to their fight date, more ghosts are going to start coming around. When they go to the dressing room or on their way out to the cage, the ghosts are going to be out there waiting for them. Each one represents a type of feeling and not one ghost is going to be missing.

I say to my guys, "You have two choices. Are you going to embrace

CHAPTER ONE | 3

them, or are you going to ask, "Do I gotta see you every time I come here?"

I tell them to talk to their feelings, like, 'You know, we're gonna be a team, we're gonna be friends. I'm gonna feel okay to feel afraid. I'm gonna feel okay to feel angry. I'm gonna feel okay to feel happy.' Whatever it is, once they embrace them, there are going to be twenty or how many ever feelings they have going on, plus all their training, up against one opponent. And if they don't do it, I say, "You're going to have to fight twenty rounds with your ghosts, get exhausted, and then also have to go out and physically fight your opponent."

So I always embrace them. Like we're buddy-buddy, you and me. It means I'm okay with you. Maybe because you made me feel bad doesn't mean I have to dislike you. Because if I dislike you, I'm the one who's losing. I know I've got to deal with you. I know I've got to face you. We've got to be together. So if I have to have you on my side or have you against me, I want you on my side.

Conan's insights about how he deals with his feelings brings us right to the heart of how to experience Emotional Brilliance™. In his own way, Conan goes through steps to nail down the answers he needs in order to win. Those steps include variations of the following questions:

- How do I prepare myself to win?
- How do I embrace my feelings and make them my friends?
- How do I show my feelings?

For the past twenty-five years, we have been teaching Emotional Intelligence (EI) to thousands of executives across Fortune 100 companies, start-ups, military special operations forces, hospitals, and federal, state, and local governmental agencies, among others. On top of that, we provide individual executive coaching, corporate training, give keynote speeches, and write books. With our podcast Leadership Development News, we have over four million listeners in more than forty-five countries, and so far, we've interviewed over four hundred top performers from whom we have gleaned best practices. We have seen what works and what doesn't on the battlefield and in the boardroom, literally.

The short takeaway about what works is a readily available and repeatable emotional intelligence process that you can get better at with practice.

NEURO TIP

WHAT IS MORE ACCESSIBLE BECOMES MORE PROBABLE

If you're thinking all this emotional intelligence stuff will blow over when the next shiny thing comes along, unfortunately that's not going to happen for a lot of reasons, the biggest one being that emotions aren't going to blow over. They are as much a part of our nature as our skin is. They're in us and around us like oxygen. They influence what we think or don't think, say or don't say, act on or don't act on whether we realize it or not. Even if you do realize the importance of your emotional life but don't take appropriate action, odds are things are not going to work out so well because the feelings left behind by our emotions aren't biodegradable.

For example, Qualtrics, in an April 2020 study of 2,000 people from Australia, France, Germany, New Zealand, Singapore, the United Kingdom, and the United States shows:

- 53.8% report being more emotionally exhausted
- 53.0% report increased feelings of sadness in daily life

- 50.2% report being more irritable
- 42.9% report feeling generally more confused
- 38.1% report increased insomnia
- 32.3% report increased anger
- 24.4% report increased feelings of guilt

In the workforce alone, the American Institute of Stress has consistently reported over the past few years that:

- 80% of workers feel their job is stressful
- 40% of workers feel their job is very or extremely stressful
- 26% of workers feel they are often or very often burned out by their job
- 25% of workers have felt like screaming because of their job stress

But this emotional distress doesn't occur in a vacuum, despite our best efforts to put on smiles. Meaning your disillusionment, and equally your happiness, have a ripple effect on all those around you. It makes sense then to try to get ahead of the wave rather than get sucked into it. If you're still not convinced on whether it's worth the time and energy to understand your emotions, let's go through some of the pros and cons.

Dr. Marc Brackett at The Yale Center on Emotional Intelligence has the following list of what emotions are good at helping with:

- Attention, memory, and learning
- Decision-making and judgment
- Relationship quality
- Physical and mental health
- Academic and life success

The website quantumworkplace.com has their own list of what emotions can help with, specifically in the workplace:

6 | EMOTIONAL BRILLIANCE™

- Performance
- Decision-making
- Employee retention
- Negotiation
- Conflict resolution
- Group dynamics
- Leadership

You can add to this research by the London School of Economics in collaboration with Jess Price Jones, founder of iOpener, which shows over 93 percent of work satisfaction is tied to feel-good emotions.

All of this means that being smarter about your emotions can have big payoffs for you at home and at work. But if it's such a no-brainer, why can't we just fix our unhappiness? That answer would be on the list of the cons to spending time figuring out your emotional life. It's a short list, but a powerful one:

- We don't know what we don't know, so things can get scary

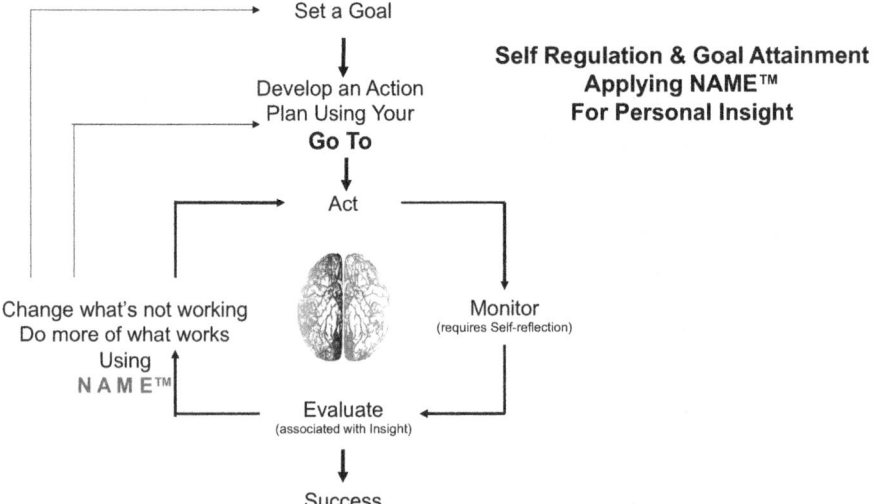

Adapted from generic model of self-regulation and goal attainment showing role of self-reflection and insight.
Anthony M. Grant, Coaching Psychology Unit, School of Psychology, University of Sydney;
John Franklin and Peter Langford, Macquarie University

One way of looking at how you might begin to understand your emotional life is shown here. It's in an adaptation of a generic model of self-regulation used to create insight through self-reflection by Anthony M. Grant and colleagues. You may want to keep this handy as a quick visual for how we can all make changes to our own personal awareness as you read through the book. You'll see it again in the Manage section of the NAME™ model.

> *"Just as we teach about good physical hygiene in the interest of good health, we now need to teach about mental or emotional hygiene too."*
>
> —THE DALAI LAMA

In a groundbreaking effort, religion aside, the Dali Lama joined forces with Dr. Paul Ekman, professor of psychology at the University of California, San Francisco and other top Western psychologists to help understand how people can learn to navigate through destructive emotional responses to possibly achieve the ideal of emotions offering a path to a calmer, more harmonious life.

The theory emerging from this research is if we can measure aspects of our emotional hygiene, why can't we create a more detailed map of our emotions to proactively channel support toward harmony or even toward the science of artificial intelligence (AI) for a vast array of growing needs.

What the Dalai Lama and Dr. Ekman have come to understand, even though they have two starkly different mindsets, is that they share common ground on how and why emotions work the way they do. Not coincidentally, we share common ground with them too in that the Dalai Lama uses the term "emotional hygiene" in regards to this research, and we use the same term in regards to the benefits of each person creating and maintaining their own emotional ecology.

Here's an analogy for emotional ecology. Just as trees are inseparable from a forest's ecology, your emotional awareness is inseparable from your emotional ecology. Your awareness is at the center of how you see yourself internally, how you see the world out there, and how you navigate between the two. It's importance now is such that measuring emotional awareness through an EI assessment, such as the Emotional Quotient-Inventory (EQ-i 2.0.), codeveloped by Reuven Bar-On and others through Multi-Health Systems, doesn't just help you get ahead as it was largely spoken of back in the 1990s, but today, a generation later, it's becoming more the norm, and so without it, you'll likely fall behind.

We're past the point of emotional awareness early adopters and late adopters—early and late ones were something we saw a lot of in the past twenty years with technology, but now the lag time between those early and late adopters has narrowed as well. For instance, there are nearly three hundred million cell phones in the US, which amounts to about 95 percent of the population having one, and we are down to the last one hundred thousand pay phones. If you are late to emotional awareness, metaphorically speaking, you're still fishing through your pockets for quarters to put in a pay phone.

This struggle to keep up is hardly new. Just look at the evolutionary time line of our early ancestors with their nomadic lives as hunters and gatherers that eventually moved into bands of social groups as agrarian communities; from there into nationwide industrial complexes that eventually gave way to today's globalized society. That we have been able to make these transformations and survive as a species is a testament to our determination for physical survival, and to our emotional survival in evolving social settings.

To illustrate this, "cave popcorn" opens a whole new way of understanding our emotional lives. For decades, archaeologists thought prehistoric art had its origins in Europe. For instance, the exquisite charcoal drawings of horses in the Chauvet caves of Southern France are a minimum of 30,000 years old. But now with advanced geological technology that can measure the decay of calcium carbonate deposits known as cave popcorn on cave walls, recent dating of a more sophisticated prehistoric drawing of a babirusa, or "deer-pig," at the Maros sites on the Indonesian island of Sulawesi shows it to be at least 40,000 years old, making it the world's oldest-known figurative art.

There are at least two major takeaways: First, archeologists are growing in confidence that even earlier art will likely be unearthed dating back 60,000 to 70,000 years ago, which is about the same period when early humans first began migrating out of Africa and fanning across Europe, Asia, and eventually the rest of the globe.

Second, the Sulawesi cave art is the first known record of human emotional connections. This artwork represents self-expression of perceptions; and with that it offers a mirror into human minds of today. Taking in life experience, processing it reasonably, and pushing it back out could be thought of as self-awareness. Of course, those cave artists knew nothing of books and seminars to be the best person they could be, however, as art scholar at the University of Western Australia, Benjamin Smith, points out, they had a distinct cognitive ability that still bridges to us: "We [they and us] couldn't conceive of art, or conceive of the value of art, until we had higher order consciousness."

Forty thousand years later, here we are still working out how to effectively deal with our emotions in the best way possible for our own well-being, and for those around us. Except now there's a new marker in our evolution. It's called Emotional Brilliance™ (EB™), and it represents an understanding beyond the essentials of emotional awareness to provide better adaptation in an evolving world. EB™ involves leveraging your best emotional competencies—your best emotional strengths and strategies—to take in the best perceptions from your own internal processing and from that of others, and then respond to the situation with your best self-expression, all in the present moment. Being able to crystalize this learning and summon it as needed is what we call your "Go To," and different situations may demand different "Go Tos" from you.

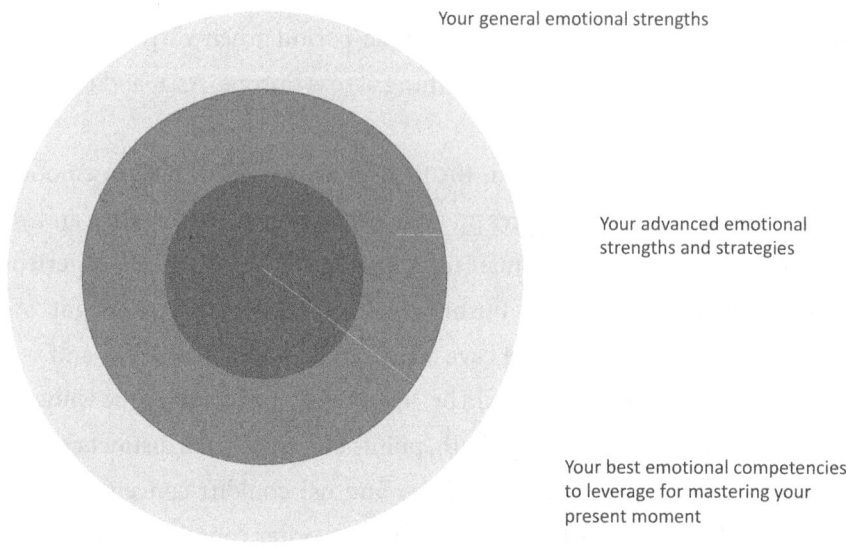

Your general emotional strengths

Your advanced emotional strengths and strategies

Your best emotional competencies to leverage for mastering your present moment

If this sounds like what you've likely heard of as emotional intelligence (EI), you're close, except Emotional Brilliance™ is EI^2; it's more accurate, more specific, and faster.

You might want to think of it this way: Emotional Brilliance™ is to emotional intelligence what a bull's-eye is to a target. A zoom lens to a camera. Or as Cathy found out, a flare on a drop zone.

It was May 21, 2007, when I took a friend for a birthday skydive with some colleagues from Navy Special Forces and Special Operations. I truly don't like to jump with civilians. Overall, they tend to be less conscientious about their skydiving, and that's a potential recipe for disaster.

CHAPTER ONE | 11

I saw too many people during my brief years of skydiving get injured by the irresponsible behavior of others practicing poor safety and canopy maintenance, and lacking experience on the drop zone.

I'd learned in life the hard way, you're less likely to have accidents if you go where the best go. So I was fortunate to take my guest to a civilian drop zone where most of the folks working had hundreds of hours in safety training and thousands of jumps under their belts.

The Arizona desert was deceptively beautiful with its sunny skies and clear views for miles. Already the drop zone was above 100 degrees by late morning. I had been told by jumpers who went before us that it was a balmy forty to fifty degrees at our thirteen thousand-feet jump height, with only a few puffy white clouds. I absolutely loved to jump through clouds. It's cool. I mean the experience was cool, but cooler in temperature too, especially in hot desert air.

Excited as always, I packed my chute, did a quick safety check, and braided my hair before grabbing my favorite red and black jumpsuit, a bandana, helmet, and goggles to gear up for a jump alongside my friend doing a beginner's tandem ride. A "tandem skydive" refers to a type of skydiving where a passenger skydiver is strapped to a harness that's attached to an experienced instructor. The two go through the entire jump together, from gearing up, exiting the plane, freefalling, and finally to landing safely.

A great way for my friend to celebrate their birthday, alongside my solo jump. Afterward, we would get a quick beverage, and I'd head for the Tucson International Airport for a program scheduled in Los Angeles.

So, there we went out of a perfectly good plane at approximately thirteen thousand feet at a cool forty degrees. The real high was always those first few moments of fast freefalling. "Don't worry," I told my friend before I jumped, "it's fantastic! It'll blow your mind. Seriously, it'll blow—your—mind!"

Well, I was right. Kind of. It did for him. Me? Not so much. Honestly, I didn't know then that when you drop that quickly from that height at a much cooler temperature and freefall into an air temperature like 110 degrees, it's like hitting a wall. I sure wish I had known that before, since I hadn't jumped for a few weeks when the temperatures were better and I was more or less "heat inoculated," that a wall of hot air could, and would, knock me unconscious.

Luckily for me, the first time I came to, I was safely under my canopy. Luckily, the cypress did its job. A cypress is an expensive little gadget you have embedded in your rig so if you hit a certain altitude and you don't or can't pull your chute yourself, the cypress automatically opens it for you.

I was safe in the sense that my chute opened, but not safe dangling in the sky, waking up disoriented, looking down and thinking first that *the ground is coming up fast* before realizing *no, I'm going down fast!* That really shocked me into consciousness long enough to position myself for as safe a landing as I could muster, knowing I was the only one who could control myself.

I took a deep breath and a second later my panic washed away. A new sense of calm washed in and allowed me to think straight. That was a huge gift, but short-lived because I blacked out again.

When I woke up this time at about eight hundred feet off the ground, it was time to line up for my dog leg landing. I remember hearing people below me yelling "Flare! Flare!" which was weird because normally you can hardly hear anything but wind when you're flying at that altitude. Flaring requires pulling simultaneously on both overhead directional lines of the parachute to slow down. But anyone who's ever been skydiving knows you don't want to flare at eight hundred feet because it's just too dangerous. What I wanted and what I needed, though, were two different things.

So I positioned my hands and started to pull. Overestimating my speed and underestimating my distance, I flared too much too soon and crash-landed. Well, crash bounced—bystanders said I had bounced on my bum so hard that the seat of my jumpsuit split wide open.

The landing wasn't pretty, but it worked. Embarrassed as much as anything else, I tried to shake off the numbness I felt from the waist down, and although it hurt to walk, I figured that was a good sign. Since I had made it through giving birth to my daughter, which lasted much longer and was much more painful, I figured I had a least twenty-four hours to get to a doctor, if I even needed one at all. I sure did.

When I finally got to the hospital the next day after returning from my overnight trip to LA, I learned why I was in such miserable pain. I'd fractured my coccyx in four places, fractured my L1 and L5 vertebrae, and caused nerve damage to my C3/4/5. It took me years to get through the nightmare of surgery and recovery, but heck I was alive, and as you can see, it makes for a great story.

After hearing me tell this, people ask if it was worth a lifetime of pain just for the pleasure of jumping out of a perfectly good airplane. "No," I answered, "but learned from it." I practice much better personal self-care these days instead of putting my health on the back burner.

I learned that when you understand how to control a strong emotion like fear or panic, you can make decisions to save your own life and get real conscious about what else you're capable of. May 21, 2007, was the day I learned how Emotional Brilliance™ works. It suspended my immediate reaction in the moment and opened a way to make my best decision in that moment. While it's not always simple, it is always profound.

Of course, EB™ rarely requires a life-or-death situation, yet how many times have you found yourself in an unhealthy situation, perhaps one where you were dealing with someone else's out of control emotions, and your feelings were intensified, and the situation demanded a reaction, hopefully constructive. Maybe like Relly did up against a big kid with a bad attitude.

I think I was only twenty-two and in my first job out of college. I had a BA in psychology and was working as a counselor at a school for adjudicated youths in Connecticut. This was the end of the line for anybody under sixteen in the state.

If you're thinking that must have been a hard situation to deal with, you'd be right. There were about twenty-five of these kids living together in this one house, and my job was to supervise them and make sure they followed all the rules. If they did break any of the wall full of rules, then they got a half-hour time-out in a small room. It was pretty aversive for me because I had lived my life up to that point trying to get everybody to like me, and in this place, as soon as I got there, half a dozen of them hated me and told me so.

So I had to make a decision. Did I want to do a good job and enforce all of the behavior modification rules, which in retrospect didn't work all that well, or did I want to let them slide on the rules so they'd like me? I needed the job more, so I went with being a disciplinarian.

There was this one student, Tony, who kept acting out, being rude to me, and disrupting the house. So I had to bust him. I said, "Tony you got a time-out for being discourteous to staff, so you gotta go into the time-out room for a half-hour."

As soon as my words came out, this big drama exploded. Just imagine bored, angry, and rebellious fifteen- and sixteen-year-olds taunting Tony: "Uh-oh, what's gonna happen now? Po' boy, you gonna take the time-out? Is Nadler gonna make you go to the room?"

The others kids egging him on definitely didn't help, but I knew something else was going on. Still, I had to draw the line: "Tony, you got a time-out. Are you goin' in?"

"You're always on my case!" he screamed at me.

I thought in that moment there weren't many choices other than doing my job, so I stepped up. "Are you refusing a time-out?" Everyone knew that refusing a timeout would get you twenty-four hours in lockup. I thought that if he was not going to go in the time-out room for a half-hour, he was sure not going to go easily to a twenty-four-hour lockup. We were both facing off, neither of us giving an inch, while more kids started gathering around to see who was going to blink.

After a minute of Tony not moving into the time-out, I said to him, "That's it for refusing the time-out, now you've got a twenty-four-hour one. If you go upstairs on your own, you'll only have to do those twenty-four. But if I have to call security, it's gonna turn into a forty-eight-hour time out."

The short answer to how he responded is: I had to call security. Two ex-cops were the security guards for the institution. They "invited" him to go upstairs, but it was pretty obvious he wasn't going to do it on his own, not with twenty-five of his peers watching. He was a tough inner city kid and had a reputation to keep. Sure enough, we had to restrain him and carry him upstairs to a room, and all the while he kicked and screamed. We finally got him there and locked him inside.

I was scared and disoriented walking downstairs with the security guards, who a moment later had to leave to go to another call. I worried what more trouble the other kids in the house, now amped up and with no other staff on duty, were going to get into. I only got in about ten minutes of worrying before I heard "Nadler!" It was Tony telling me he needed to go to the bathroom.

So I go back upstairs, let him out, and wait. When he's done, as he's coming out of the bathroom, he says, "I'm not goin' back in there."

I go, "What do you mean you're not going back in there?" My confusion, anxiety, and fear started to build up more.

"I'm not going back in, and you can't make me."

That really made me anxious and scared. It was another standoff. But instead of calling for the security guards again, I put my hand on his shoulder to lead him back to the room with its thick door and a big two-by-four bracing it.

As was sometimes the case with these kids, if you touched them, they shoved you back. So Tony said, "Don't touch me again." He was a big kid, probably 250 pounds. I had played football in high school and college and was fitter than him, so made a split-second decision to go at him. I got him in a headlock and wrestled him down the hallway until we both fell into the room. The unspoken understanding was whoever got up first was going to lock the other one in. But I was quicker than him and won that round.

I was relieved, confused, and regretful that I had to use force to get him in the room. Also, I felt somewhat proud that the event was over. I went back downstairs where the other kids were playing pool and still jacked up from all the excitement going on with Tony.

Another fifteen minutes went by, and I smelled smoke coming from upstairs. Tony, still locked in the room, had lit his mattress on fire. It turned out he'd hidden some matches and decided to burn the place down even though he was locked inside. I got him out and sprayed down the mattress with a fire extinguisher.

I thought a lot about that experience afterward. Tony trying to burn the place down while locked inside the room was such a profound statement about his inability to handle his anger toward me. But I was no genius either in not being able to handle my own emotions better. So we both made unfortunate decisions. I would later understand that both of us experienced an amygdala hijack.

This was a major life lesson for me in seeing the consequences of feelings getting out of control.

The risks for anyone to not know about their feelings, their triggers, and how those affect their decisions, and then to not know how to manage them, really hit home for me.

---

1. What stands out for you in Cathy and Relly's stories?
2. What is one thing you learned that you could apply to your life?

NEURO TIP

HOW YOU BEGIN INFLUENCES HOW YOU END

Experiencing a malfunction after jumping out of an airplane or becoming aggressive against better judgment are examples of something called an amygdala hijack, a term popularized by Daniel Goleman, PhD in his book *Emotional Intelligence*. The brain's amygdala is activated when we feel overly stressed. As a result, it takes over the executive functioning part of the brain, or our rationale thinking, and we temporarily behave with fewer IQ points. That's especially a problem when we keep doing the same unfortunate thing without learning, which makes understanding and managing our hijacks all the more important.

The combined degree of your threat, fear, surprise, past experiences, and subsequent release of stress hormones trigger an emotional hijack in the autonomic nervous system. Once it's activated, it sets in motion a rapid release of hormones in the limbic system of our brain that speed directly to the spinal cord and almost instantly causes an immediate reaction generally known as fight, flight, freeze or faint.

These four possibilities are the body's urgent call to action when feeling threatened. The perceived size of the threat is crucial to determining the best survival response in that moment—so feeling mild fear will barely get a rise out of you, but feeling terrified certainly will. Your survival response, though, isn't just random. Your body's muscle groups store information from your previous hijacks, like emotional bookmarks, which are then catalogued as feelings that ultimately create your unique patterns of automatic reactions when you're under pressure or in fear or pain. Neuroscientists tell us, "Neurons that fire together wire together." More simply, you'll keep doing the same thing until you figure out a better way; which is really the story of life. Knowing what to do with your feelings can help you have a better story.

The study of the human brain and human behavior, and most recently the mind-body connection, have been a focal point of medicine since the days of ancient Greece. The field has grown to include leadership studies in which Dr. Warren Bennis, lovingly known as the "Father of Leadership" studies, holds a special place and demonstrates many of the Emotional Brilliance™ competencies.

> *"If knowing yourself and being yourself were as easy to do as to talk about, there wouldn't be nearly so many people walking around in borrowed postures, spouting secondhand ideas, trying desperately to fit in rather than to stand out."*
> —WARREN G. BENNIS, *On Becoming a Leader*

Dr. Bennis (1925–2014) was a first-class observer, and parlayed that trait into a prolific career as a pioneer in the contemporary field of leadership studies. He counseled American presidents, American mom-and-pop businesses, and those in-between. He was known for many things, but mostly for his idea that successful leaders demonstrate integrity, compassion, and a unique capacity for sharing their power through collaboration, motivation, and inspiration by observing and inquiring rather than by telling or selling. That concept was out of sync with the mainstream when he started writing about it in the 1970s considering top-down authoritarianism was held up as the ideal for strong and successful leadership. But today, his teachings serve as a foundation for leadership practices and are taught in business schools and management programs around the world.

He's also not just an abstract famous thought leader for us, there's a personal connection. Bennis was one of Cathy's lifelong mentors:

> Warren and I collaborated on several ideas close to his heart including "networked leadership" and "great teams" featured in his books like *Organizing Genius* with Patricia Ward Biederman, and *Geeks and Geezers* with Robert J. Thomas and Dee Hock.
>
> During one of our visits, he dedicated a book to my dad: "From one father to another," he wrote in June, 1999. Sadly, the book missed my dad by one day. Dad passed away on the day the book arrived.
>
> Warren also introduced me to many great minds like Howard Gardner, Edgar Schein, Margaret Wheatley and David Gergen through the Harvard Kennedy School and Cape Cod Institute. And Marshall Goldsmith, which led me to working on the largest study of its kind using the Global Leadership 360 Assessment. We measured the skills and competencies that global leaders need in order to succeed, and it turns out that emotional awareness is what lets the genie out of the bottle, or as Warren called it, "personal mastery" in a humanistic and democratic-style environment.

Bennis was prescient because today you would be hard-pressed to find many people succeeding with blinders on, unaware of themselves and of others. Even in the military, where the way leaders run their commands can make the difference between who lives and who dies, understanding our emotional lives is just plain practical.

General Robin Rand (Ret.), Commander, Air Force Global Strike Command and Commander, Air Forces Strategic—Air, US Strategic Command

> It was the fall of 2005, and I was getting ready to go to San Antonio for a four-day conference. I was a colonel then, stationed at Luke Air Force Base just outside of Phoenix where I was serving as commander of the 56th Fighter Wing. Shortly before departing for the trip, one of the squadron commanders assigned to the 56th Fighter Wing named Bryan Harris came up to me and asked, "Sir, if you have time when you're in San Antonio, one of our Airmen was seriously injured in a car accident and is now hospitalized at Brooke Army Medical Center in San Antonio. Could you go visit him?" To which I replied, "Of course, Bryan, count on it."
>
> This young man was named Senior Airman Kevin Close, and he had recently returned from a deployment in Iraq. Happy to be stateside again, he started out on a road trip to visit his girlfriend. Except he didn't get there. No fault of his own, he was in a terrible car accident and lost one of his legs just above the knee.
>
> While I was at the conference, I remembered Bryan's request and went up to my boss, General Looney, and said, "Sir, if at all possible, I'd like to miss tonight's event to go see a young Airman from Luke who's in the hospital recovering from a very tragic car accident." General Looney, a great leader who passionately cared about our Airmen, answered "Of course, Baba, please pass along my best regards."

CHAPTER ONE | 21

The 56th Fighter Wing Command Chief Master Sergeant Scott Dearduff, my spouse Kim, and Chief's spouse Mags, made the thirty-minute drive and found Kevin and his father in one of the hospital rooms that would be his home for the next several weeks.

Upon seeing us, he had this look on his face like, "you are the last people I want to see right now," but when he saw our wives with goody baskets filled with cool stuff, his demeanor seemed to warm up. We talked and got to know each other a bit, and after a few minutes, I recall Kevin asking if he could have a picture taken with Command Chief Dearduff and me.

I said, "Definitely, it would an honor." So, Chief and I started to squat down to get eye level with Kevin sitting in his wheelchair, when he said, "Nope...no sirs, I'm not going to be sitting down for this picture." He asked his dad to hand him his crutches, and stood up on his one remaining leg. It had only been a couple of days since his surgery and I could tell by the way that he became pale and flush, that this was zapping a tremendous amount of energy out of him. But, I also sensed that his actions were a way of saying "I have my dignity and I'm going to stand for this picture, regardless of how badly I feel."

About then I decided it was time to go because I could see that Kevin was worn out by these "unexpected and uninvited intruders!" That's when I also realized something: his dad had been standing quietly in the corner of the room the whole time.

"Before we go, I want to give your father something," I said to Kevin. It was what we call a commander's coin, and like many commanders, I gave coins out rather spontaneously to express gratitude and/or recognition. At that moment, it seemed so appropriate to present Kevin's father a coin. This coin wasn't flashy, but it had several distinguishing features that symbolized the 56th Fighter Wing's legacy from World War II, and on the bottom of the coin in Latin was engraved the 56th's motto *Cave Tonitrum* which means, "Beware of the Thunderbolt."

While I can't remember my exact words, I remember explaining the significance of each of the details on the coin and then saying something to the effect of, "Sir, I want to thank you. We appreciate the love you show Kevin, and while he's your son, he's part of the 56th Fighter Wing. Please accept this coin as a token of our gratitude for taking care of someone who is also part of our Air Force family."

Without missing a beat, Kevin's dad said, "Colonel, while I appreciate your gesture, my son deserves this coin far more than me." I remember chuckling out loud and saying, "Sir, with all due respect, it doesn't work that way. You don't get to give away this commander's coin. So how about I give Kevin his own?" At which point I did, we then said our farewells and departed.

The ride back to base was very quiet as the four of us reflected on how this young Airman would certainly be facing an uphill climb in the weeks and months ahead.

Shortly after my wife Kim and I got back to the hotel, she turned to me and said, "You know, it wasn't until tonight that I realized how much power you have." We'd been married for twenty-six years at that point, and I sarcastically said, "Honey, I've been trying to tell you that for the last twenty-six years."

Kim was not laughing and with tears welling in her eyes, said, "Did you see the look on Kevin's face when you were giving the coin to his dad? He had this look . . . one of true appreciation and gratitude."

"Honey, it's no big deal," I said.

Like only someone who had witnessed most, if not all, of my character flaws could say, Kim, quietly, but firmly, looked me straight in the eye: "Yes, it is a big deal. You impacted him in a profound way, and tonight I fully realized how your position affords you the opportunity to make a simple, but positive difference." Then she paused for a second before adding, "So don't mess it up."

Since that night in October 2005, I have thought many times about our visit with Kevin and his dad. I have also reflected on the wisdom of Kim's sage advice. She was right. It is a big deal being in a position that allows you to make a difference. Being a commander can and does result in making a difference, good or bad. I'm also mindful that absolute power "can corrupt absolutely." Most important, I've learned that any power and authority that comes from a leadership position, if harnessed properly, can result in making a positive difference!

As a leader in an organization, in my case the United States Air Force, my power came strictly from the position I was temporarily afforded the opportunity and privilege to serve in. I missed the mark more than a few times over forty years of leading. However, throughout that journey, it was clear that the key to ensuring that my power and authority didn't become detrimental or self-serving was to remain mindful that I must always do my best with the authority I carried. When done right, I was able to support the mission at hand, while taking care of the Airmen and their families under my charge. Thank you, Kim, for reminding me of this, and thank you, Kevin, for showing me why we serve.

---

1. What stands out for you in General Rand's story?
2. Have you done anything lately that's worth being remembered for?

Honor, dignity, gratitude, and our other feelings usually occur instantaneously in response to our emotions. Usually feelings happen to us, we don't happen to them. However, by coming to understand them, we can have more influence over them and reduce tendencies to be self-defeating. While all emotions are natural, equal, and okay, inappropriately expressing the feelings borne from emotions is not okay.

Take sadness, for example. It's natural to feel sad when someone leaves us or suffers or dies as many people have during the COVID-19 pandemic. But if that sadness extends beyond a natural and healthy expression and turns into inconsolable grief or self-pity, then that's a problem. This is an important distinction and worth repeating. All of our emotions are natural; what's at issue is when we inappropriately express them. In short, emotions = always good; expressions of them = it depends. Knowing this distinction underlies Emotional Brilliance™.

The United Nations might not be the first place you'd think of for insights into your emotional life, but in the spring of 2019, our friends at Six Seconds invited us to a groundbreaking inaugural program at the UN designed to do exactly that.

The conference focused on the implementation of emotional awareness to support a variety of populations, including those with mental health and trauma-related issues in war-torn countries. Its basis was to take a global approach to treating one person at a time, kind of like being an "Ambassador of Human Beings." Kind of an initiative that someone like Mr. Ramu Damodaran, the United Nations deputy director for Partnership and Public Engagement, could dig into.

While working at the United Nations, I always look at situations to determine a physical response: send humanitarian workers to an emergency; send peacekeepers into a conflict; get diplomats into a negotiating room to come to a settlement on a dispute. But I don't always realize there is, as a famous writer once put it, the space within the heart, which is really critical to all of this. That space is where my emotions are not something to shy away from, but are something I can cherish and recognize and mold, and are not completely sequestered within myself, but are extendable and shareable.

So if I have an emotion that is very joyous and lighthearted, and I communicate this to a person, it could either work for the good, or it might make the other person think I am frivolous. And similarly, if I express an emotion purely within the space of my own being, I might sometimes find myself inadvertently either exaggerating or minimizing a situation. To put it more simply, I think emotions are instinctive. But nurturing them and harboring them is not. For that, I need reflection and time.

As an example, I experience every day something that is probably becoming a little out of fashion: simple affection. When I am walking down the street and see a mother coming with her eight-month-old child, I instinctively lean over and smile at the baby. But I don't instinctively lean over and smile at someone my age, or younger, or older, so I make an effort to do so. Every time I see someone just catch my eye, I give a smile back and walk on. It brightens my day, and I hope the same thing for them.

I can also be creative without suppressing my natural indignation, or anger, or sadness because those are emotions I must recognize and accept, but not allow to be destructive.

One of my responsibilities at the United Nations is something called public engagements. That is engaging the public with the United Nations and all that it stands for. I have sometimes thought that it was a slight misprint because what I sometimes feel is a sense not of engagement, but of enragement. I get enraged by so much that is happening in our world today that is within human capacity not only to address, but to forestall. That essentially becomes, in many ways, my negative reaction. A reaction of frustration. What I try to do then is translate my sense of personal enragement into a collective resolve to action. Talk about it, write about it, show the absurdity or the injustice of it, to get people to come up with emotionally intelligent resolutions.

Whenever I wake up and see all that has happened in the world over the past twenty-four hours—and I'm talking about very positive things, I'm not talking only about the sad, depressing, and negative things, just all that we have seen within our grasp and all that is possible—I realize my whole identity is that of being an emotionally stable human being, and an emotionally receptive human being. I think, above all, an emotionally caring human being.

---

1. What stands out for you in Ramu Damodaran's story?
2. What matters most in your life and how do you show it?

"Recognize stress as an untransformed opportunity for empowerment."
—Doc Childre

Colonel David Grossman, author of *On Killing* along with other books on the warrior's mindset, has an interesting perspective on violent video games and their influence on young people in what he calls the "Assassination Generation." First, he believes we can take what we learn from the battlefield and apply it to our own neighborhoods. In Colonel Grossman's words: "Systematic examination of the individual soldier's behavior, like all good scientific theory making, leads to a series of useful explanations for a variety of phenomena."

He says that what makes soldiers kill or not kill will continue to be a topic of crucial importance, if not for national security reasons, then at least for a better understanding of whether there is such a thing as a "natural born killer." It's clear that most of us are not, but we can become unnatural and kill.

NEURO TIP

WE CAN INJURE OUR BRAINS WITHOUT KNOWING IT

Colonel Grossman has spent decades training soldiers, police and others who keep the peace, and he researched how they overcome the intrinsic human resistance to harming others. Drawing on crime statistics, cutting-edge social research, and scientific studies of the teenage brain, he ties some teens' increase in antisocial, misanthropic, and casually savage behavior to an emotional buildup far outside their normal life to be a result of them playing violent video games. What's interesting is that many military troops in the field use video games for just the opposite reason—they play them as a release and for sport to decrease their aggressive behaviors and to bring them back within the emotional comfort zone of their normal life.

This both-sides-of-the-same-coin dilemma is exactly the kind of inquiry that leading-edge researchers like Rudolph Tanzi in his newest book *The Healing Self* with Deepak Chopra, and Doc Childre in *Overcoming Emotional Chaos* with Deborah Rozman are trying to untangle.

Doctors Childre and Rozman, in particular, address emotional stress using their HeartMath™ user-friendly, affordable software and video tool.

They start by asking some compelling questions:

- Does who you care about drain you or energize you?
- Are you compromising yourself or taking advantage of others just to make it through the day?

- Is what you care about stress producing or stress reducing?
- Do you believe that letting people know how you feel will leave you vulnerable and likely to be hurt or taken advantage of?

There's a lot we can learn from the HeartMath™ model, not the least of which is that some emotional stress is healthy. In fact, there's a word for it: *eustress*; it was coined by the endocrinologist Hans Selye who added the Greek prefix "eu-" and it literally means "good stress." For instance, fear to keep you safe or anxiety to keep you motivated are often innovational as in Plato's "Necessity is the mother of invention." At least, that's how Rotem's mother sees it.

Debby Elnatan, Israeli mother and inventor of Upsee, a walking aid for disabled children

> Rotem is our second son. When he was eight months old, we found out that he had cerebral palsy. Actually, we were called into a school and told, "Your son doesn't know what his legs are. He has no consciousness of his legs." That was an incredibly difficult thing for a mother to hear. I cried probably for the first week or two.
>
> In time, I understood that Rotem's sitting in a carriage was not going to get him far. So disobeying his therapists' recommendations and behind their backs, I started to walk him day after day. If we went to the playground, I had Rotum walking.
>
> As I helped him up the steps to go down the slide, I just remember the feeling of all the other mothers' eyes on me when their kids were just playing naturally. I imagined them feeling sorry for me, but I probably mostly felt sorry for myself. And my back hurt from bending over. It's very hard to walk a two-year-old because you're

down on your hands and knees practically on the floor. And I just said, "There's got to be a better way to do this." Out of my pain and desperation came an idea.

Because my dad was so handy, I had learned to respect people who worked with their hands. He would give me tools as presents, and until this day, I have a ratchet set he gave me so I could fix my own car. He gave me a big gift that enabled me to respond to many situations, making it often easier to just create what I need. I think there's a common thread between America and Israel. Self-reliance. My dad was very American, and he taught me self-reliance.

So I tied Rotem's ankles to my ankles and put a strap under his underarms and held him. He took three steps and then collapsed. But by the end of the year, we could walk two hours. Then I went on to sandals. I asked around in Jerusalem, "Who can help me build these double-sandals?" And I was pointed in the direction of Uri, a professor of shoemaking! We worked together to make these sandals. Then I worked on the harnesses. It was a long process during which I also got to know what motivates my kid.

You have to learn your child, or they have to learn you. Are you going to start out together on the right foot or the left foot? How fast are you going to go? There's a physical bonding, and then there's something else. Who's taking the lead? If you let your child take the lead, they almost forget that you're there behind them.

Even though he's not an independent walker, my role as a parent is to be there behind him, to give him support; enough so he can do what he's able to do. To let him feel like he's the roller and the mover. To let him think about what he can do, rather than what he can't do. To help him explore the world around him, to reach out and touch. To help him establish his personality, his place in the world.

My hope is that Upsee will be used all over the world to give our children a better childhood.

---

1. What stands out for you in Debby Elnatan's story?
2. When did you last push the boundaries of your comfort zone?

CHAPTER TWO

"Life begins at the end of your comfort zone."
—Neal Donald Walsch

Each of us puts on our own emotional magic show by pulling rabbits from hats, turning clubs into hearts, and making coins vanish when it comes to what we feel, how we perceive those feelings, and how we express them. We are masters of illusions with our thirty-four thousand distinguishable feelings, even when we simplify those down to Plutchik's primary eight: joy, sadness, trust, disgust, fear, anger, anticipation, and surprise. As examples, you can refer to the body of research on emotions, or to the world's foremost researcher on lying Dr. Paul Ekman's one-liner: "People also smile when they are miserable." Or, you can ask George what he thinks.

George Piro, FBI special agent in charge of the Miami Field Office and former Assistant Director of International Operations, DC Headquarters

> I learned a lot about my own emotional well-being from a stone-cold heartless dictator. The "Butcher of Bagdad" was our FBI team's target for a year before his capture in a grubby underground hideout in the town of ad-Dawr, Iraq on December 13, 2003. About a week and a half later, on Christmas Eve while on my way to the mall for

last-minute gifts, I got a call telling me I had a new assignment in Iraq. I was an FBI special agent at the time and soon to become the lead interrogator of Saddam Hussein.

Forget about all you've heard on beating confessions out of hardened criminals and sociopaths. It's not even half as effective or reliable as building a rapport, an emotional connection, with the subject. I drew great inspiration from then Senator John McCain. Senator McCain had said that whenever the North Vietnamese tortured him when he was a POW during the Vietnam War, it didn't break him, it strengthened his resolve. So we didn't waterboard Saddam or electrocute him with cables connected to a car battery, we understood what made him human, treated him with respect and helped him reveal to himself and to us what made him feel emotionally vulnerable.

Through the seven months I came to know Saddam and he to know me, I found a deeply disturbed man, and perhaps he found in me someone who could help him relieve some of his loneliness. I don't for a moment think he felt remorseful for the hundreds of thousands of innocent people he ordered to be murdered—I know he didn't because I asked him.

Instead, he was a man consumed by his legacy. In his demented mind, he saw himself as a historic figure who would be celebrated a thousand years from now. The present or even the immediate future was of no interest to him, he wanted to be immortalized, and this character flaw proved to be his undoing.

We all know now that his threats with weapons of mass destruction were bluffs. We know now he had no WMDs, they had been destroyed by the UN inspection teams, and what few remnants turned up were destroyed by the Iranians. And yet Saddam brought his country into war against the US and our allies rather than admit he wasn't the strongman he had portrayed himself to be. In private, he eventually allowed me to see the weak man that he was. One who couldn't tolerate criticism and who had to always be right.

He loved his mother and was angry that his father had been mean to him. He was disappointed in his two sons, Qusay and Uday, both reported to be more ruthless than him, saying of them at first that they had good relations but eventually admitting, "You don't get to pick your kids. You're kind of stuck with what you get."

The times he showed this ordinariness surprised me the most. Deep down, he had the same basic needs all of us do. To feel loved and to enjoy the companionship of others. He even cried when we said our goodbyes as he was being prepared to transfer from US custody into Iraqi custody and face trial for his crimes.

I believe justice was served with his execution. Yet, despite my close involvement in gaining his confessions and then helping the Iraqi courts prosecute and sentence him to death, I have watched the video of his hanging only once. I think that's because it is disturbing for me see that happen to someone I knew on an emotional level.

---

1. What stands out for you in George Piro's story?
2. When all is said and done, what will you have done more than you've said?

The Müller-Lyer illusion is a good analogy for understanding more about how we fool ourselves. Though you probably don't know it by name, you've likely run across this optical illusion many times before and by now know that all of the lines below are exactly the same length, even if the middle one with the arrowheads facing outward appear to be the longest. The leading explanation behind this mind trick involves perceptions and perceptual processes that occur continually, automatically, and unconsciously when you take in stimuli, drive it through your neural highway, identify it, and take action on it; in this case, the common action is to conclude that the middle line is the longest.

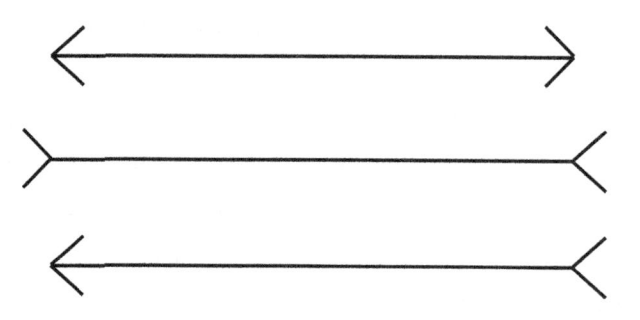

Though there's no such thing as a Müller-Lyer-like diagram for emotions, there ought to be because your perceptions and perceptual processes that occur continually, automatically, and unconsciously also shape your emotional life. For example, anthropomorphism is when you give human traits to nonhumans; like holding the common belief that dolphins are happy animals because they appear to always be smiling. Add to this dolphin mix the theory of emotional contagion, which mostly says that what others feel will spread and influence you and those around you to feel the same way, and you can see your emotional self-assessment will probably be tricked in a similar way as the middle line in the Müller-Lyer illusion does.

It's not the dolphin's fault that you perceive their beak-like rostrum curving up at the ends and supported by a long jawline to be a smile, especially when this structure is entirely anatomical and has nothing to do with their emotions. In fact, dolphins can't make any facial expressions. Their "smiles" are borne solely from your own emotional perceptions.

You can think of this as mirroring, and if others pick up on it you can think of it as contagious. With the dolphin example, no one gets hurt. But unfortunately, if we mirror emotional negativity and it spreads, it can be more harmful than many contagious physical illnesses. Meaning, if you catch the common cold or a flu virus, it will die off eventually, but if you hold on to hard feelings, they will live on. If you're not sure about this, riding out a Category 4 hurricane might be more convincing.

Rob Marmerstein, chief operating officer at HCA Houston Healthcare Kingwood

> Early in my career, I had an experience as a young administrator where I dealt with a situation in a way that I thought was appropriate, and it turned out that somebody who was not involved in the situation really made some pretty inflammatory accusations as to my lack of empathy or appropriateness. I was at first taken aback and offended and angry. I really felt attacked and resentful. And I was scared.
>
> I was almost ready for an argument with this person until I talked to a few of my mentors and was able to calm down. *Okay,* I thought, *maybe I was misinterpreted and perceived as being judgmental versus collaborative,* which is what I was trying to do. I asked myself, *what's my desired outcome from this situation?* Well, my desired outcome couldn't be the natural course of, "Oh, I want revenge."
>
> Instead, I made it okay with myself by saying: *I think I've suffered an injustice. It's a drag, I don't like it, but I've learned from it and will be a better person moving forward because of it.* So I shifted my own emotions and really let the rest slide. Although I didn't feel like that was fair, that was the best outcome for me.

At the end of the day, it's, "what is my desired end, and am I progressing toward it or away from it?" When I fall into the trap of getting kind of emotionally hijacked and having these feelings of retaliation and other negative things like that, I am not progressing toward my end, I am progressing toward something that makes the baser parts of my brain feel good for a couple of seconds and that's about it.

That lesson was really important when Hurricane Harvey hit in 2017. Although everybody knows what they sign up for when they work at a hospital, when they actually made the call and I had to come in during an emergency situation, all these other emotions really came up.

I came into work that Friday with my air mattress and a couple changes of clothes and didn't go home until the following Thursday. I was worried about my family, pets, and loved ones in the area. Worried about whether my house was still there. Worried that I couldn't be with those folks because I need to take care of patients. I had to remain focused on our patients even though there was a lot of fear and anxiety around. I thought, *Well, I'm here, and I really have to make the personal sacrifices.*

Communication was so important. It just filled some holes of uncertainty with real information in order to keep calm and feel safe. I think we all know in the absence of information people tend to make up their own stories and those are usually negative or scary ones, right?

Toward the end of the storm, I hadn't slept very much for four or five days. Nobody had. Nobody was really at their best, and this one nurse was very stressed out. She was being positive, but you could just look at her and tell she was kind of at the end of her rope. Someone walked up to her and said, "I think you need a hug," and put her arms around her. I could feel the entire room change. That one little five-second piece of human-to-human warmth absolutely took the tension out. It was really moving to watch that. Yeah. A hug goes a long way.

---

1. What stands out for you in Rob Marmerstein's story?
2. If you had one piece of advice to share from your life, what would it be, and how could you share it?

NEURO TIP

MANAGING YOUR FEELINGS AND HELPING OTHERS MANAGE THEIRS MAKES FOR GOOD RELATIONSHIPS

With the Müller-Lyer illusion, you can always pull out a measuring tape and verify that the lengths of all three lines are exactly the same. But getting quantifiable verification for your emotional self-assessment isn't as easy. For example, use your imagination and see the abstract drawings below as representations of your fear:

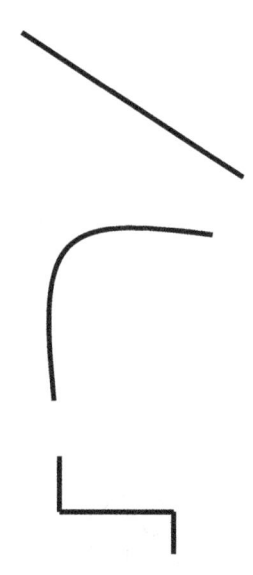

Despite this illusion that the fear is different, all three fears are the same (all three lines are the same length). Only the depictions, the expressions, are different. One drawing could represent you appropriately asserting yourself; another you internalizing; and the other you being passive.

This brings us back to one of the central themes of Emotional Brilliance™. All emotions are equal, but the many ways they're expressed are not. So how can you figure this out other than the hard way? With the Emotional Brilliance™ questionnaire.

EMOTIONAL BRILLIANCE™ QUESTIONNAIRE

RATE YOUR ANSWERS: 1 = STRONGLY DISAGREE, 2= DISAGREE, 3= NEUTRAL, 4 = AGREE, 5 =STRONGLY AGREE	SCORE
1. I notice when I am experiencing sensations in my body	
2. I know and can name what I am feeling almost all the time	
3. I am able to accept my feelings even if they are unpleasant	
4. When challenged, I am able to summon my best "Go To" strategy for the situation	
5. I know which "Go To" strategies to develop more	
6. I have many action strategies to manage my feelings	
7. I have many thought strategies to manage my feelings	
8. I can express my varied feelings easily	
9. I feel heard and accepted when I express my feelings	
10. I can let go of feelings and move on once expressed appropriately	

CHAPTER THREE

"For it was not into my ear you whispered, but into my heart. It was not my lips you kissed, but my soul."

—Judy Garland

In an ironic twist of homonyms, love found its home in "hate"—Haight-Ashbury that is, more often just called the Haight—when in the Summer of Love in 1967, a reported one hundred thousand mostly young people flooded that San Francisco bohemian neighborhood to find themselves, individually and as a generation. Their outpouring was infectious. Complete strangers helped one another: Kids with all of their worldly goods stuffed into backpacks found places to crash for free. They shared a free community food bank. A free community medical clinic. Free music. Free clothes.

Haight was a rejection of all America had known itself to be: an uptight, capitalistic, white-dominated, gender-siloed farm with its conformist citizenry of sheep willingly allowing themselves to be herded into open pastures or closed pens depending on the vagaries of the establishment. As Deirdre English, then a teenager who had travelled from New England to San Francisco that summer, writes:

> The attitude was one of seizing life, feeling free; feeling that if we do not like something, we can change it; feeling there was this critical mass of people who wanted to reject inherited, authoritarian, conformist ideas and make the world our own.

Indeed, many at the epicenter of the Summer of Love—the cool ones—saw themselves in just those terms as rejectors of a social order that was out of touch; while those on the outside—the square ones—saw themselves as protectors of that order. But the revolution turned out to be much deeper than that. The Beatles and The Rolling Stones, growing long hair and tie-dyeing shirts, burning draft cards and burning bras, and "turning on, tuning in, dropping out" were only affects of the times: the real revolution was about emotional expression. From the Mission San Francisco de Asís to the Missionaries of Charity in Calcutta, the call went out to lend a hand and make a difference.

Monsignor Michael Mannion of the Camden Archdiocese

> I sat on the bench a lot. I mean, when I was a kid and wanted to play sports, I didn't get on the field much because other kids on my teams were better than me. But that bench warming gave me time to think. I came to realize that there are a lot of people who sit on the bench but still have a lot to offer, and by the time I entered the priesthood I also came to realize that the most able aren't always the ones who get recognized.
>
> I kept thinking about this and eventually founded what we call Discovery House for kids. In a big way, it's for kids who've been benched. Now, after forty-five years, we've helped forty thousand people get off the bench and out onto the field.
>
> Discovery House provides structure, retreats, and other programs to help them see that sometimes what they think is strength is weakness, and what they think is weakness is strength. Like when they think the strong don't cry, even though tears are purifying and releasing and provide an openness for greater understanding of themselves and of humanity.

We help them understand there are lessons we learn by heart, and lessons the heart will learn. So I can have a match and drop it to the ground and burn down the house, or I can put that same match in the fireplace to warm the house. That's a lesson of the heart.

I'm truly fortunate to have had the privilege of working beside Saint Mother Teresa to help care for Calcutta's poor off and on for at least twenty-five years. She referred to her people as the unwell, the unwanted, and the unloved. It was a blessing to be a loving correspondent during her funeral and an honor to sit among her beloved sisters throughout her canonization at the Vatican in 2016.

In Calcutta, both the poor and Mother taught me many lessons of the heart, but everybody mostly wants to know what she was like. I can tell you that she created a world using the extraordinary gifts God gave her, but that she only saw herself as ordinary. She thought what she did was something everybody could do. She had the view that everybody was equal, which helped me be better able to piece together an understanding that while our functions may be different and our results may be different, our equality of soul remains a constant.

Mother thought everybody could help one another with a smile and the gift of love. She made me smile with her good sense of humor. One time, we were seated next to each other at a ceremony honoring her. After she received the award, one among so many, she jokingly whispered to me, "Now I can open a plaque shop."

She also always went for the transformative experience, in part by seeing things in people that they didn't see in themselves, me included. After I became a priest, I felt called to serve the poor and so reached out to Mother Teresa to ask if I could join her in her missionary work. I asked her, "If I come, will you put me up?" She answered, "Yes, but don't come," and then went on to explain that

Americans were dying in our own streets. That was true, but I didn't listen to her and went anyway.

After serving in Calcutta with Mother for some time, I asked if I should stay on and she said, "No," and her explanation this time was because the United States had a poverty of the soul.

Two of the biggest lessons I brought back are that when we recognize this isn't about me, then we can conquer our demons; and that ego is a resource and not an identity because maturity is not about success, it's about significance. It's not about getting where we want to go by using people and loving things, it's about loving people and using things.

---

1. What stands out for you in Monsignor Michael Mannion's story?
2. What does the difference between success and significance mean to you?

Saint Mother Teresa's remarkable life brought her canonization as a saint nineteen years after her passing. So many others who held themselves to the highest standards of humanitarianism received their own rewards in life, and remembrances of them continue to this day, not as saints, but as ordinary people who did extraordinary things by lending a hand. Like Eleanor Josaitis, affectionately known as "Detroit's Mother Teresa."

Noel M. Tichy, top management consultant, bestselling author and educator shares this story

One of the most heroic leaders I have ever had the pleasure of working with was a woman who has passed on now. Eleanor Josaitis was

CHAPTER THREE | 45

the cofounder of Focus: HOPE in inner city Detroit. After the riots there in the late '60s, she gave up her comfortable life in suburbia and moved her family right into the heart of where the riots had broken out and helped build an organization that was dedicated to intelligent, practical solutions for racism and poverty.

Focus: HOPE now has a full Detroit campus with a children's center, vocational training for machinists and electricians, a bachelor's program in engineering, and a food program for those in need.

Yes, she was *one of the* most heroic leaders but *the* most inspiring I have ever, ever worked with. I think that's because Eleanor was willing to look in the mirror every day and ask, *what can I do to add value to the people in the community?*

There's this one video clip where she's up in front of 450 students, and she says to them something like: "Let me read you some of the love letters I've gotten." A lot were far from love.

Eleanor held up one of them so the students could see for themselves. It was a newspaper article in *The Detroit News* about her life's work, and across it in black felt-tip pen was scrawled a violent vulgarity. "If anyone in this room thinks for one minute I'll be intimidated, you are wrong. This only makes me work harder. We have to work together to end the terrible racial bias that exists!"

When I was at Eleanor's deathbed, she said something that I felt then was very unfair, but now feel is wonderful. She said, "You must carry on the work." I look in the mirror every day and think about her words. That's why I set up the Eleanor Josaitis Citizenship Initiative at the University of Michigan and fund projects all over the world in her name. I've also worked nationally with Boys and Girls Clubs and YMCAs. Those organizations, as well as the Boy Scouts and Girl Scouts, rely a lot on volunteers.

When you become engaged in volunteer work, it changes you as much you add value to the institutions. So I encourage people, whether it be with your church, synagogue, Boys and Girls Clubs, YMCA, or somewhere else, get out there and give back. You will gain more in life by doing this and get your emotional compass adjusted while you're at it.

Another one of my most important things is to have a small network of people I can be absolutely candid with about where I am. To share my doubts, fears, and hopes with. Because I can't say I'm going to help other people without being willing to look in the mirror at myself and get some tough love from those I trust. I've got about four or five people like that. And it goes both ways, I help them as well. We find each other invaluable. I'm sure there are many times I would have walked off the edge of the earth if some of them hadn't woken me up and said, "Hey, stop! You're full of it and need to think about this."

This kind of emotional awareness is necessary. It starts with being very clear with yourself, and from there, to begin to look at your own needs on where you would be wise to develop more and how you're going to get there.

---

1. What stands out for you in Noel Tichy's story?
2. How would you like to honor someone's work so it lives on?
3. How would you like others to honor yours?

Thousands of miles away on the other coast during that same summer of 1967 in San Francisco, a fledgling scientific understanding of emotions was facing its own resistance and staging its own revolution. Among those rebels was a twenty-four-year-old named Jaak Panksepp, a promising graduate student working toward his PhD in psychobiology/neuroscience from the University of Massachusetts, Amherst.

Up through the 1950s, behaviorism was the king of the hill for describing how the human psyche worked, and its leader was the then legendary and today iconic Harvard psychologist B. F. Skinner. According to Dr. Skinner and the mainstream scientific community, which predominantly came from the school of behaviorism, emotions mostly did not matter in life. To the upstart Panksepp, that view reeked of brutality and denial because emotions were not to be treated as one would in breaking a horse's spirit in order to train and ride it.

In a 2012 *Discover Magazine* interview, Dr. Panksepp was asked how he had managed to survive against those giants of science. "I learned to bite my tongue until they couldn't hurt me anymore," he answered. "I bit my tongue many times, but not hard enough usually. So gradually, I became a radical without wishing to be a radical."

But for someone who rose to be such a monumental figure and whose work still heavily influences us to this day, it is a bit funny that he was perhaps most well-known as the "rat tickler." During the course of his career, he had conducted research that proved rats laugh. Their laughter is expressed as an ultrasonic joyful chirp. This seemed silly to many, and he caught a lot of ridicule for his "breakthrough." But it bore out to be a significant discovery for a number of reasons.

One, he dared to plant a flag in behaviorists' territory ruled by very smart men of the establishment. His would become one of many flags along with Paul Ekman's and Robert Plutchik's that within twenty years would unseat behaviorist theory altogether.

Two, he wholly dismissed the notion of human exceptionalism, which essentially said humans were at the center of the universe (the very smart men of the establishment offered themselves up as proof), and as the only sentient beings, humans were the only life form with emotions; to which Panksepp replied: "People don't have a monopoly on emotion."

Three, he helped contextualize emotions as being universal and described how, "despair, joy and love are ancient, elemental responses that have helped all sorts of creatures survive and thrive in the natural world." Which meant a person in Phoenix fundamentally had the same emotional framework as someone in Tapei or Johannesburg or Lima, and fundamentally the same as a bird or elephant or cat.

And four, those very smart men of the establishment who had been siphoning away from research grants into studies that challenged their position on the irrelevance of emotions would eventually lose all their funding to this opposite research on the relevance of emotions.

Panksepp famously went on to identify seven neural networks of emotions that originate deep within brain structures. Those seven are SEEKING, RAGE, FEAR, LUST, CARE, PANIC/GRIEF, and PLAY. That these seven are in all capital letters is not a typo—he considered them to be so foundational across all animal species that they deserved this special spelling.

Just a few miles from the Haight during the Summer of Love, a twenty-nine-year-old PhD named Paul Ekman stumbled his way into the revolution that Panksepp had more deliberately engaged in. Years earlier, Dr. Ekman had been offered a federal research grant to study nonverbal communications. He had not sought it and had no particular interest in the subject, however, as a matter of practicality, it provided him with a salary for nine years and then further provided him with a research budget for the next thirty-one years to augment his full professorship at the University of California, San Francisco. The year 1967 proved to be pivotal in producing even more insights—Ekman along with his research partner Wallace V. Friesen discovered micro facial expressions of emotions.

This revelation would launch Ekman into the history books along with blueprints showing that unlike obvious facial expressions of emotions that usually last for up to four seconds and match the emotion being conveyed—both truthful and deceptive conveyances—there are micro expressions that are revealed as, "very brief facial expressions, lasting only a fraction of a second. They occur when a person either deliberately or unconsciously conceals an emotion. These revealing facial expressions are universal, can't be prevented and often occur without our knowledge."

This type of facial recognition is valuable in at least three primary ways:

It can help you read your own emotional state better so you have fewer, in Ekman's words, "regrettable emotional episodes."

It can help you read grifters' emotional states better so you understand that, in his words, "certain people just don't make mistakes when they lie. These are not just psychopaths but also natural liars."

It underscores we all share the same set of emotions—in 2016, Ekman realigned that set to be comprised of just five: enjoyment, anger, fear, sadness, and disgust.

Back in Long Island, New York during that Summer of Love, psychologist Robert Plutchik was busy at work on his next scholarly book to be published the following year, and was developing diagnostic tools to assess emotional states. More of an obscure scientist in 1967, Dr. Plutchik unknowingly was laying the foundation for what would become in 1980 his Theory of Emotions and move him from the shadows into the spotlight.

His theory states that people and animals are all in a psychoevolutionary process—or in simpler language, emotions evolve over time just as bodies and minds do, and for the same basic reason: so the species survives.

Humans don't always require a major evolutionary event like an ice age to become stronger or more suited to the environment. More often, only a behavioral change is needed, just as we are doing now in response to the application of new technology, like using cell phones for so much more than just communication

For instance, just watch two teenagers sitting next to each other and giggling while they stare at their smartphones. Or remember when you were first struck by someone walking down the street talking passionately to seemingly no one only to realize they were using a hands-free phone?

These are examples of a more recent evolution in social norms, which ultimately have had an impact on behavior through the emotions and feelings we now share in public, including those by people who lack awareness and have private phone calls that invade public spaces. Thus, many of our socially acceptable and unacceptable behaviors continue to evolve as our social interdependence evolves.

Looking to the past, we also only needed behavioral changes to adapt to major cultural shifts, like developing more social skills in moving from nomadic hunters and gatherers to community-centered farmers.

In hindsight, Plutchik's approach makes perfect sense, but in his time, he was quite the revolutionary—and if proof of that was needed, he had embraced the work of fellow rebels Doctors Panksepp and Ekman. Of the ten postulates to his theory, these three are directly tied to the Panksepp-Ekman rebellion:

1. The concept of emotion is applicable to all evolutionary levels and applies to all animals including humans.
2. Despite different forms of expressions of emotions in different species, there are certain common elements, or prototype patterns, that can be identified.
3. There is a small number of basic, primary, or prototype emotions, such as fear.

For example, Cathy's understanding of emotional awareness, and the more elevated Emotional Brilliance™, is informed by her PhD studies at Rutgers University as a physical anthropologist and behavioral scientist. This includes her being influenced by world-renowned primatologist H. Dieter Steklis who believes the basic list of recognizable primate emotions hasn't changed that much. What he says has changed, though, is our ability to explore the emotional conditions under which those expressions consistently appear.

Another world-renowned primatologist, Frans de Waal, has spent nearly three decades studying chimpanzees, and more recently, has drawn conclusions about their emotional lives. One is that they're a lot like us, or depending on your point of view, we're a lot like them.

We both show our emotions—fear, amusement, sadness, anger, disgust, and others—on our faces and in our postures. We both understand to varying degrees empathy, sensitivity, protectivity and other nuances in emotional responses.

Dr. de Waal even thinks great apes and monkeys may experience a sense of fairness. In his book *Mama's Last Hug: Animal Emotions and What They Tell Us about Ourselves*, he describes an Emory University study of capuchin monkeys (commonly known as "organ grinder" monkeys) that demonstrates their complete satisfaction when all of them were given cucumbers as a treat, up until some of the monkeys were given sweet grapes instead. The disparity caused all hell to break loose. Those given cucumber slices became angry, apparently outraged over the unfairness of not being given the better treat. Which begs the question, is their sense of fairness or envy inherent, or is it learned?

Either way, whether they are consciousness of their own emotions is one of the most complicated answers to figure out. If we view dogs, dolphins, chimpanzees, or other nonhuman animals as able to experience consciousness, what does that mean for us? It's a spiritual, philosophical, and ethical dilemma about a presumed human superiority over animals and how we interact with them.

For example, de Waal tells a story in *Mama's Last Hug* about fellow scientist Jan van Hooff saying goodbye to Mama on her deathbed due to natural causes. While she laid in her bed, he approached with her permission, with cameras capturing every moment. As Dr. van Hooff looked into her eyes and reached out, she wrapped her arm around his neck while patting his back and caressed his face like a mother would with her own child, which then led to their eventual last hug.

In this final exchange between two colleagues, human and nonhuman, a clear and deep connection existed between them. Whatever our catalogue of the core prototypical emotions is, one thing is certain. Recognizable qualities of emotions can cross between humans and nonhumans. To what degree remains a mystery, but to even explore it requires Emotional Brilliance™.

Where Panksepp had determined there were seven primary emotions and Ekman five, Plutchik had determined there were eight.

PANKSEPP	EKMAN	PLUTCHIK
Rage	Anger	Anger–Fear
Fear	Fear	Sadness–Disgust
Panic/Grief	Sadness	Joy–Anticipation
Lust	Disgust	Trust–Surprise
Care	Enjoyment	
Seeking		
Play		

And unlike his colleagues who saw emotions as stand-alones, Plutchik saw them as pairs, or more accurately, pairs of opposites: joy versus sadness; anger versus fear; trust versus disgust; and surprise versus anticipation. All interacting and influencing each other with varying intensities—for example, rage or anger or annoyance—in ebbs and flows throughout life. To illustrate his theory, he created what is now famously known as Plutchik's Wheel of Emotions shown below.

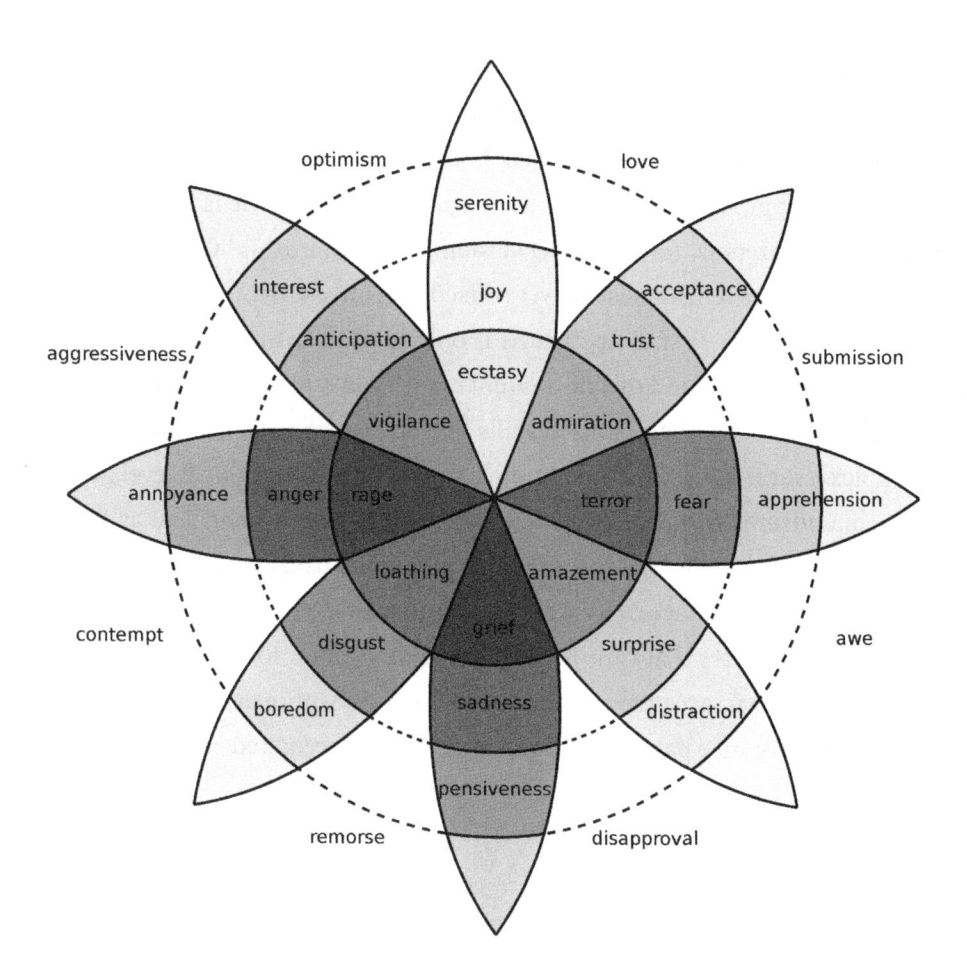

[Plutchik's wheel of emotions diagram showing: optimism, love, serenity, joy, interest, acceptance, anticipation, trust, aggressiveness, ecstasy, submission, vigilance, admiration, annoyance, anger, rage, terror, fear, apprehension, loathing, amazement, contempt, disgust, grief, surprise, awe, boredom, sadness, distraction, pensiveness, remorse, disapproval]

Doctors Panksepp, Ekman, and Plutchik's models of emotions still carry a great deal of influence today, including in the otherworldly field known as "affective computing," which involves integrating emotion-based behaviors with artificial intelligence (AI).

Obed D. Louissaint, the gracious and inspiring former director of AI Healthcare Technologies, IBM Watson, and currently IBM's Global Vice President, Talent, focuses on his company's investments in some of the fastest-growing segments in the information technology market. He also leads the human resources efforts for IBM Analytics, Commerce, Security and Research, IBM Watson, Watson Health and Waston IoT.

His position clearly requires strong administrative and organizational skills, but it also requires equally strong people skills, which he applies using a servant leadership approach. It will come as no surprise then that he is known for his empathy, awareness, foresight, persuasion, and stewardship. Oh, and a great smile, all wrapped in a polished, yet relaxed executive style.

He is one of the first to say that AI is only as good as the people who know how to use it, and to add that no amount of tech can replace talent. AI can handle many high-order mechanized skills to help free up people to handle more complex issues. But what it cannot do is connect on an emotional level, which is a conundrum when computers are being rolled out as smart and as fast as possible to take on more of the work that people are usually assigned to.

Obed has somewhat of a workaround for this: first empower people systems and people cultures that can then stimulate innovation for more AI applications. Rather than accepting a blurring of the lines with machines, he holds a distinct unassailable passion for people's emotionallycentered relationships.

NEURO TIP

YOUR FEELINGS INFLUENCE YOUR DECISIONS

Other new research has also been significant in shaping effective paths to Emotional Brilliance™. In particular, research confirming that emotions are different from feelings. This is not just about choice of words; it's about understanding how the brain works.

Emotions are biological sensations that occur almost instantaneously and arise from the deepest parts of the brain—primarily in the hippocampus and amygdala—commonly referred to as the reptilian brain. This reptilian term is meant to tie emotions we live with today to emotions that originated in prehistoric times—emotions that are often counterproductive to us, like hoarding things beyond reason due to a nagging fear of scarcity.

At its core, the reptilian brain is about survival of the species, and when survival is on the line, as many of us have found out in our own lives, we check, double-check and triple-check because mistakes have consequences. For example, you don't need to be alert for saber-toothed tigers like our ancestors were, but that same prehistoric safety-check feeling today alerts you to not drink milk that smells sour.

Feelings, however, are the responses to emotions. If emotions are from the Stone Age, feelings are from the Space Age. In a practical sense, you cannot rewire historical emotions, but you can do a lot to rewire present-day feelings. You can even hone your optimal responses to situations by resting on and applying your key strengths and capabilities—the practicality of this is at the heart of Emotional Brilliance™.

As Lisa Feldman Barrett writes in *How Emotions are Made*:

> We construct our experience and perception of emotions from the bodily sensations our brain receives, using our internal model of the world. Our internal model of the world is constructed from past experience that is organized into categories, or concepts. The brain uses these "concepts" to "categorize" sensations so as to give them meaning. As humans, we categorize everything to help us make sense of the world. They are cognitively laden. And these categories, or concepts, influence our behavior.

What this means more simply is that Dr. Feldman Barrett sees the brain as a predictive machine converting emotions into feelings as a way to try and keep us safe. "Try" being the operative word here because predicting the future is a risky bet.

Other new research shows that emotion-based neurochemicals last in the human body on their own for about six seconds. This brief pause is the sweet spot because that is when you can help or hurt yourself in shortening or lengthening those six seconds. This depends in large part on how emotionally adept you are at interpreting your situation, processing your internal feedback, and then responding favorably. This is an example of Emotional Brilliance™.

Josh Freedman, CEO of Six Seconds, is one of the world's preeminent experts on emotional intelligence. He believes that six seconds is usually all the time you have to share your emotionally intelligent superpowers, like interpersonal and problem-solving skills, to be flexible in today's volatile, uncertain, chaotic, and ambiguous world.

His easy-to-find website www.6seconds.org shares everything from free research like the annual "State of The Heart" to pop-up programs for children of a generation needing more advanced coping skills. Six Seconds also offers assessments for life and business enhancement through coaching tools and cafés. For those who want to go further, Six Second Certification programs include an array of online, virtual, and in-person workshops with their amazing Brain Apps™ to demonstrate how "serious science is made simple," accessible, fun, and memorable.

NEURO NOTE

Six Second Brain Apps™ include drivers such as Emotional Insight, Connection, Collaboration, Proactivity, Risk Tolerance, and Imagination.

Their Brain Brief™ distills "the power of an advanced assessment tool into one page of quick, meaningful insights, and provides snapshots of your brain's style and talents to effectively use emotional + cognitive data."

Unlike many style inventories, their SEI Brain Profiler™ suite of tools is derived from a full-power psychometric response and assessment that is then analyzed with a special algorithm utilizing twenty normative scales backed by decades of research.

Their Brain Profiler™ suite of tools includes three individual reports and one group snapshot for easy reference. Check out the different profiles to find out how your unique style, strengths, and challenges affect your life.

Accessing these tools gives you a real advantage, particularly when it comes to being engaged. In business, managers foster an environment of regard for one another in what is called employee involvement. In medicine, providers bring patients and their families into what is called shared decision-making through patient-centered care. And in local government, officials stress transparency and hold open town hall meetings in what is called public participation. In each case, they are trying to get you to "buy in." But it turns out you're not for sale, which is why, despite a steady increase in incentives, a Gallup poll reports that only 33 percent of Americans identify as being actively engaged in their work.

So what is going on with the 67 percent who are not engaged? The short answer is that they're just not into it. The long answer is they do not genuinely feel that their inherent or developed sense of emotional positivity, like excitement or enthusiasm, is welcome.

A recent study of nearly forty-five thousand employees that was published in the *Journal of Organizational Behavior* validates that emotional positivity is the single strongest predictive trait of engagement, far more than other predictive traits including being proactive, conscientious, extroverted, and agreeable.

Separately, industrial-organizational psychologist Dr. Dan Harris concludes that those who are comfortable with constructively expressing their emotions, whether it be sadness, anger, happiness, or others, have the highest levels of engagement in their work, and significantly more than the levels of those who are uncomfortable with expressing themselves.

British-based EBW Global has been applying similar methods as Harris through their Business Emotional Intelligence assessments and certification. It consists of eight main emotional behavioral clusters: Decisiveness, Motivation, Influence, Adaptability, Empathy, Conscientiousness, Stress Resilience and Self Awareness. Senior Partner Stephen Walker says this is a practical approach to helping individuals and teams understand why people behave the way they do, and how to maximize that understanding.

NEURO NOTE

Check out EBW Global's website at www.ebwglobal.com to learn more about their tools for leadership development, diversity and inclusion, cultural transformation, attracting and retaining talent, as well as their practitioner network based on six continents.

Now, more than fifty years since the Summer of Love, a larger set of laws of emotions and feelings has emerged. Below are some of the stand-outs:

LAW OF FEELINGS
1. Emotions are electrochemical signals and data that flow through our bodies
2. Feelings are the mental experiences interpreted from these bodily sensations
3. Feelings are contagious and influenced by rank/title and power/influence
4. Feelings range from pleasant to unpleasant; intensity ranges from low to high, negative feelings are stronger and stickier than positive feelings
5. Naming your feelings helps reduces their intensity
6. The less you know about your feelings the more you will project them onto others
7. Repeated feelings create an emotional bookmark
8. Feelings aren't biodegradable—they can contaminate you and your thinking
9. Replaying negative feelings injures the brain—it can destroy memory and emotional regulation
10. Feelings need to be experienced and accepted to manage through them, they want to get out and get over

Sources: Damasio (2018), Newberg and Walkman (2014), Luckner and Nadler (1997)

This last point about brain health makes a strong argument for letting go of grudges. Refusing to forgive is about the same as taking poison and waiting for someone else to get sick from it. Michael Vick has something to say about that.

Michael Vick, former NFL record-breaking quarterback and sports commentator. Convicted felon for dog fighting.[*]

> We're all human and we all make mistakes. It's scary when you first go in and you don't know what to expect. Anybody who doesn't come from that type of lifestyle, or has never put themselves in a position where you can be sent off to prison . . . you know, I couldn't adjust, I couldn't relate. But I did because your goals and your ways of thinking are always more vibrant when your back is against the wall. First of all, you're sitting in the cell and you're asking yourself, "Who do I blame?" I blame me. "Why am I here?" I knew why I was in there. Every day I was hurtin' and cryin' and my heart couldn't take it anymore. And you feel like the scum of the earth.
>
> It was life-changing because I had to get to know more about myself personally, and the everyday challenge of pushing yourself to take your mind outside of the prison. I had so many people in there who supported me and pushed me to be better, pushed me every day. As crazy as it may sound, and I know it's ironic, I always tell people I wouldn't change that part of my life for anything because I learned so much about people, so much about myself. I can't speak

---

[*] As a result of this dog fighting conviction over twelve years ago, forty-seven dogs rescued from Michael Vick's dogfighting operation lived. They've enriched the lives of countless humans and altered the course of animal welfare. As victims, the rescued animals are now provided with rehabilitation services. Those that cannot be adopted may live their lives without fear of abuse in peace.

for other people, but I just came out a better person. I came back more of a people person, and I respect that more than anything.

More understanding, more loyal, more trusting. I always knew I needed that. I always wanted to be a person who wasn't shying away from the big opportunities and the rooms that I could be around, and the people I could be around. I always shied away from that. I thought I didn't need it. It's like, man, I gotta take advantage of some of the great things that God has put into my life.

I understand the forgive-but-not-forget mentality. That's supposed to be logical and the way we're supposed to live. But I can't. I can't hate you because you've committed a crime. I can't do that. Now there are a bunch of things that I don't believe in, and there are a bunch of things I do believe in. But when somebody breaks the law, I can't hate them for it. I don't know the reason why they went through that, and they don't know the reasons why I went through what I went through. So I forgave myself at the end of my prison sentence.

Just know that I've done everything in my power to make amends, and I'll continue to do that for the rest of my life because it's a lifetime commitment.

As a result of this dog fighting conviction over twelve years ago, forty-seven dogs rescued from Michael Vick's dogfighting operation lived. They've enriched the lives of countless humans and altered the course of animal welfare. As victims, the rescued animals are now provided with rehabilitation services. Those that cannot be adopted may live their lives without fear of abuse in peace.

---

1. What stands out for you in Michael Vick's story?
2. To what degree have you really controlled the course of your life?

CHAPTER FOUR

"No one cares how much you know, until they know how much you care."

—Theodore Roosevelt

Just off of the 101 North, about forty miles shy of the Oregon border, go east on Arrow Mill Road past Crivelli's Bar and the Star Mobile Home Park, cultural symbols of the most powerful nation on earth, and drive deeper into the remote forest of two thousand-year-old giant redwoods cocooning the twenty-two-mile stretch of Red Mountain Road snaking its way to the once-powerful but a now nation of invisible people. The Yurok, California's largest Native American tribe with about six thousand members, is one of the few indigenous tribes in the United States still living on their ancestral lands. They survived the Gold Rush, timber rush, and salmon rush, and today are fighting to survive the addiction, drop-out, and incarceration rushes.

For all of the reservation's old world mysticism in which they view the now plentiful king salmon running through the Klamath River as family, just as they do the Roosevelt elk grazing on rare oak grasslands, they also live with old world pragmatism in which they view meting out justice to be more about emotional healing than about punishment.

This native Indian approach that began Americanization in the 1970s under the name of restorative justice has spread today to New York, Los Angeles, New Orleans, Duluth, Boulder, Baltimore, Chicago, Minneapolis, and Seattle, and to a growing number of counties, cities, and parishes throughout virtually every state in the nation.

"There's got to be truth and there's got to be forgiveness ... Or we stay attached to that anger and stay attached to that hate," says Judge Abinanti. "We have had to look really deep within ourselves to do the forgiveness, and I think that will make us stronger as a people." Abby Abinanti's long gray hair drifts elegantly across her shoulders to almost the middle of her back. She wears her usual judge's attire, not the black flowing robe we are used to seeing our judges in, but gray jeans, a black cardigan over a turtleneck, and one of her favorite pieces of jewelry, which is quite often a white dentalium shell necklace or hand carved redwood earrings.

Judge Abby, as she is called, has been chief judge of the Yurok Tribal Court since 2007, following a distinguished career as the first Native American woman to be admitted into the California Bar, serving as a litigator in private practice, and retiring after twenty years as a San Francisco commissioner ruling on family law cases—cases that are most often emotional battle grounds for hurt, distressed, and traumatized mothers, fathers, and children.

Also, unlike the elevated benches from which she and others in the US hold court, she sits at a modest table that is at eye level with everyone else: "We're trying to create a place where you can come and figure out a way to get your life back to harmony, and can be in community without dispute. We live around each other. All of our ceremonies are large family gatherings. You're on the river with hundreds of people, you have to get along."

What Judge Abby had learned in San Francisco opened the door to her reclaiming her Yurok heritage and reintroducing an ancestral judicial system to her tribe that was more compassionate, while also placing more responsibility on the perpetrators and their victims for healing relationships based on a communal sense of Emotional Brilliance™. The Indian belief is not that everything can be reconciled—some things are just plain wrong and can't be made up for; however, healing is always possible if the people commit themselves to it. The main difference is reconciling needs emotional awareness, while healing needs Emotional Brilliance™.

In an array of Native Indian traditions, these processes almost always take into account all injuries to the involved individuals' families. For example, in some instances of an accidental death amongst the Aleut (Eskimo) or Lakota tribes, holistic healing might include the individual who caused the death to marry the widow left behind and ensure that her family is cared for, or for the individual who caused the death to be adopted and to take on the burden of the lost person's responsibilities. True healing requires a broader view to the cause of the injury or harm beyond the visible.

Much like the healing tradition of Native Indians, we are all searching for the causes of our individual pain beyond the visible through our feelings of anger, fear, anxiety, loss, and grief.

Thus, Emotional Brilliance™ can be key to healing.

In part, this is because we often stand on the foundation of science winning out over power and fear. In this case, the science is rooted in our own power to face our fears, understand them, NAME™ them, and gain insights into them to make ourselves more adaptable, happy, and satisfied.

This ability to see the bigger picture in general is something all of us have had to get used to in dealing with the pandemic beyond 2020. Specifically looking at the bigger picture to become more emotionally well-rounded, though, first gained momentum in 1990 when Doctors Peter Salovey and John D. Mayer came up with the term Emotional Intelligence for an article they wrote— it is also referred to as EI, or EQ as a spinoff of a person's cognitive intelligence, or IQ. They described this as "a form of social intelligence that involves the ability to monitor one's own and others' feelings and emotions, to discriminate among them, and to use this information to guide one's thinking and action."

A few years later as the buzz about Salovey and Mayer's work picked up credibility, prominent people like Dr. Daniel Goleman and Dr. Richard Boyatzis lent their names to the movement, and soon what had been only a stream of support became a river with Goleman's 1995 book titled *Emotional Intelligence: Why It Can Matter More Than IQ* leading the way. His book sat on *The New York Times* bestseller list for a year-and-a-half, was translated into forty languages, became an international bestseller, and helped spawn a whole industry that bridged personal development with personal finance.

His revolutionary way was not so much *Think and Grow Rich*, with which Napoleon Hill had attracted millions of followers, but rather "Feel and Grow Rich." Having intellectual smarts was good, but having emotional smarts too was a better bet to end up successful. Goleman's evidence was so compelling that it legitimized a balanced approach between emotions and business and consequently sent a hush over those who had been drinking the corporate American Kool-Aid spiked with "emotions have no place in business."

Having been influenced by Goleman's work during her postgraduate days at Rutgers, Cathy combined her experiences across primatology, business, and the behavioral sciences to spearhead the work of integrating personal mastery, consciousness, and emotional and social intelligence in her own books on the science of happiness, quickly followed by the science of courage.

He is also cochairman of The Consortium for Research on Emotional Intelligence in Organizations, originally based in the Graduate School of Applied and Professional Psychology at Rutgers University, which seeks to catalyze research on best practices for developing emotional competence and its impact on leadership and organizations.

Dr. Goleman's conclusions can be summarized as:

- Getting an understanding of your emotions will pay off as much as getting an MBA.
- Leading and managing your own emotions is essential to leading and managing others.
- Empathizing with other people's emotions gives you more career opportunities than bulldozing through them.

These early views on emotional awareness have largely proven to hold up over time, and today the beginning stream of acceptance that turned into a river has now turned into an ocean filled deep with sister movements like mindfulness, meditation for stress reduction, resilience, and change your brain to change your life practices. One of the things that has helped emotional awareness hold its own as a separate discipline is the remarkable number of new discoveries about emotionality that keep reinventing its purposefulness. Those discoveries are applicable to social justice and business as we discussed, and also to just about every area of life from being a better boss or more loving partner, to living healthier and enjoying life more.

NEURO NOTE

Learn more about how you can listen to interviews with these thought leaders and about the release of the New Emotional Intelligence Coaching Certification from Dr. Daniel Goleman at www.eblifebook.com.

If you're not sure where you land on the emotional awareness scale, there are literally dozens of assessments available. In addition to Six Seconds's widely adaptable methodology or EBW Global's business-focused program as we've discussed, there are other tools more often used by psychologists, professional coaches, and therapists including the Emotional and Social Competence Inventory (ESCI), Multi-Health Systems Emotional Quotient-Inventory (EQ-i 2.0), and the Mayer-Salovey-Caruso EI Test (MSCEIT). All of these are available through professional certification.

The validity of many other assessments is improving, though there are still a number that do not have enough supporting research to back them up.

NEURO NOTE

Check out the international-based Consortium for Research on Emotional Intelligence in Organizations at www.eiconsortium.org for more information. It's the *Consumer Reports* for these tools by providing objective quantifiable evaluations, as well as serving as a clearing house for the latest on developments in the science of emotional awareness.

TAKE ACTION! To get started, you can go to www.eblifebook.com and take our online EI Star Profile and the Derailer Detector to identify the competencies and which ones you want to do more frequently to improve your results.

Regardless of which assessment you use, there are two key points to keep in mind. First, there are no right or wrong answers; they are just your answers. In fact, accepting where you are without judgment is an indicator of emotional awareness.

Second, this is a process, not an event. By practicing at it, over time you will increase your aptitude for emotional awareness in the present moment, and that will put you in a whole different arena. Moving naturally from emotional awareness to Emotional Brilliance™ is discovering your artistry as if you're composing music like CeeLo Green.

CHAPTER FOUR | 69

CeeLo Green, five-time Grammy Award-winning recording artist, music producer and entrepreneur

I got into an awful lot of trouble growing up in Atlanta. I may have always been aware of my artistic talent, but I lacked an outlet, something formal or constructive, so I became destructive. Music saved my life. The voice you hear, the soul, the pain, is that of a person who deeply, deeply, deeply appreciates the opportunity they've been given. I've not always known myself completely, but if you look at where I was when my first big hit, "Forget You!" came out, hopefully it's evident I've grown up quite a bit now.

We had to clean up the song some and put it out as "Forget You!" which helped push it to the top of charts around the world. It's good, but doesn't have the same intense anger as the original lyrics with profanity in them.

Most people think the song is about a girl. In a literal way, it's about a girl. The storyline is a fictitious account of love lost. But it's a trial that we've all been through at some time or another, and I think that's why people can relate to it. I mean, not literally, at least not for me. Like the lyrics, "Yeah I'm sorry, I can't afford a Ferrari / But that don't mean I can't get you there." Then I couldn't, but now I could afford to buy a Ferrari.

But when I was writing it, the message came from someplace different. I'd been recording for three years and I had over seventy songs, and I was ready to be heard. But my label was just sitting on it, and it was very disheartening not knowing if what I was doing was good enough. It seemed like I couldn't please anybody. So of course, figuratively I was like, "You don't like me? Well forget you!" It was very cathartic.

Then a year later, I recorded a new version as a tribute to America's volunteer firefighters. I renamed the track "Thank You" and altered the lyrics so the chorus now goes: "For a lifetime of service in the name of love, we wanna thank you / I could say it a thousand times and it wouldn't be enough, we wanna thank you for everything you do."

I connect with it very, very personally because my mother was a fireman as well—one of the first black female firemen in Atlanta, so quite a historic accomplishment. It's a convenient means for mixing the song and using that same spotlight to acknowledge and expose what a great humanitarian cause so many people, citizens, volunteer themselves for. It's not by force, it's not by draft. Theirs is all heart and soul.

So for me, I took the song from my deep anger all the way to my deep gratitude. I think it's imperative that people be able to be enlightened by what my inspiration was for a song, the actual origins, but then for that song to take on its own life for individuals. Because I believe that you should individually interpret music and the emotions it brings you and make it applicable to your own experience or see it the way you want to see it. That's the art in full context.

---

1. What stands out for you in CeeLo Green's story?
2. Which is worse, failing or never trying?

CHAPTER FIVE

"Start where you are, use what you have, do what you can."
—Arthur Ashe

Marshall Goldsmith, business educator, coach, and bestselling author

Many years ago in 1984, I was a volunteer for the American International Red Cross and went to Africa on a famine relief campaign. People there were starving to death. I'd never seen a person starve. In America we talk about starvation, but this was different. This starvation was when there's no food in the garbage cans. I actually saw people licking blood off of the concrete because that was the best they could do for nourishment. I was there for nine days and saw many people die. It was such a gut-wrenching experience that made me realize how lucky I am and what really matters in life.

In my book *Triggers* I have a picture, there's only one picture in the book and it's of this trip to Africa. It shows me down on the ground next to a woman. She's kneeling down and measuring the arms of little children waiting in a line. As it turned out, they only fed children between the ages of two and sixteen because they didn't have enough food for everyone. If they tried to feed everyone, they'd all starve to death.

She was measuring the arms of these little children and if their arms were too big, "they're not hungry enough so they go over to 'A.'" If their arms were too small, "they're going to die anyway so they go to 'B.'" And if their arms were in the middle they actually got food, which meant they had a chance to survive. It was called triage.

I have that picture in my library and I try to look at it every day when I'm at home. It reminds me to be grateful.

Be grateful for all you have. That could have been you, could have been your children. Those people are just as good as you and me, so remember there are many people in the world who don't have the blessings we have. Just have gratitude.

When I came back from Africa, I was all full of myself. I was thinking, *I'm a great humanitarian,* and *I'm on the cover of the local newspaper,* you know: "Yuppie thirty-two-year old humanitarian goes to Africa to save the world and isn't he wonderful."

My friend Dr. Sam Popkin had a nice little welcome back reception at his home for me. He got up and bragged about what a great person I am. I was feeling full of myself for being such a good deed-doer. I was talking to a small group of people and they're all listening to me pontificate. Then the group kind of faded away and finally there's just one old man left, and I said to him, "I'm sorry sir, I didn't catch your name."

He looked at me very humbly, "My name is Jonas Salk." I felt like such an idiot and went, "Oh my God" because I was so full of myself and thinking I'd done so much, but here's the guy that cured polio.

It's good to demonstrate humility in life and realize no matter how wonderful we think we are, there are a lot of other people who have done a whole lot more for the world than we could ever imagine.

CHAPTER FIVE | 73

So first, we need to express gratitude, and second, we need to realize maybe we're not quite as wonderful as we think.

---

1. What stands out for you in Marshall Goldsmith's story?
2. How will you live knowing you can do more for yourself and others than you're doing now?

Knowing what to do with your feelings and how to interact in support of others is critical for your own well-being, for your community and workplace, and for the global healing required to thrive in the new normal of a post-pandemic world. It's integral for "Building Beyond Better" (BBB), as New York Governor Andrew Cuomo phrased it. What the governor foresees post-pandemic is more large-scale change in our already quickly evolving world, such as more virtual practices and tighter airport security.

On the brighter side, BBB is expected to offer a quick uptake of software apps and technology for improvements in health, education, service, and business. The positive results will likely include faster access to telehealth and medicine with less travel, and more time with those who matter the most to each of us, including your ninety-seven-year-old aunt who finally understands the magic of Zoom.

NAME™ provides support through its simple formula that can give you more robust, timely, and rapid personal insights. You'll learn how to better understand and name your feelings to gain more clarity about the roots of your emotional triggers, which in turn will make it easier for you to develop healthier "Go To" options for facing your daily challenges. While most of our adult learning experiences take place privately within ourselves, you'll also find this process offers up emotional awakening from your interactions with others, and with nature.

The connection between nature and emotional awareness is well-known, but it really only started to gain scientific traction here in the US in about the 1950s. A decade later, psychologist Erich Fromm came up with the term "biophilia" to describe a love of all that is alive, and world-renowned naturalist E. O. Wilson took the idea even further in the '80s, in part by specifying a love of the environment.

What has followed are exciting new ideas about being in nature as a way to promote emotional development. For instance, the art of forest bathing emerged in the West, a concept that originated in Japan and is known there as *shinrin-yoku*. Its purpose is to calm nerves, resolve internal conflicts, and restore emotional balance. Blue Mind science applies the same principles, only instead of forests, its orientation is on bodies of water—an ocean, a lake, a river, a swimming pool, a bath—to bring about greater emotional awareness. Those who love the mountains or deserts report on similar effects.

Today, as a result of the pandemic and the social distancing it requires, more people are turning to gardening as a way to experience their emotional lives more fully in the absence of person to person connections. Soleil Ho, the *San Francisco Chronicle* restaurant critic expresses herself this way: "I posted a photo of my chives growing the day after I found out my friend died of COVID-19 in Brooklyn, and I thought, *what is the point of any of this?* But at the same time, to see something persistently alive . . . it's something that just wants to live, and to me that was really touching."

Artist Alex Testere describes what it means to him to have built a trellis on which he grows beans: "Feeling stuck and stagnant, you just can't go anywhere; you feel a tremendous loss of control. I think the thing I've always found with a plant is you can take care of it and watch it transform, and maybe it becomes something you can even eat—that's just such a powerful force of positivity in a time when that's hard to find."

Whether it's the destructiveness of a virus or wildfire, the extinction of an animal species or an infestation, the vast expanse of the galaxies or a delicate sea breeze across your skin, the sound of ocean waves breaking or the smell of

CHAPTER FIVE | 75

tall woods—however you allow yourself to experience the full force of natural forms in their harshness and beauty, eventually that will lead to your insight and clarity strengthening and pay dividends. Despite all of these easy-to-access benefits, many still don't go outside enough.

Richard Louv writes in his monumental book *Last Child in the Woods*, that we are experiencing far less of this nature-bountiful wellness and instead are mired in a "nature-deficit disorder" from being glued to our computers, overscheduling our days, and living with the realities of urbanization stripping away natural settings for gentrification.

If you like to crunch numbers, the Environmental Protection Agency has some: The average American spends 87 percent of their life inside at work and home, plus another 6 percent inside their cars, for a lifetime total of 93 percent spent indoors. That amounts to only 7 percent of an average American's entire life being spent outdoors. Clearly that's a problem in itself for overall wellbeing, but specific to this book, it creates a lot of emotional logjams.

Here's the thing: For all of the talk about emotional awareness, it's when you take action based on this awareness that you can break through jams and lift up your emotional awareness. With even more awareness and action, you can achieve Emotional Brilliance™. For example, taking action to spend more time outdoors is just one of the many action steps in the NAME™ model.

Notice and name your feelings
Accept your feelings
Manage your feelings
Express your feelings

NAME™ can serve as a GPS for navigating your feelings and also for helping and supporting others. We developed it based on other distinguished models that help us move from thinking to doing. These other models include the original work of Mayer, Salovey and Caruso on identifying the abilities to perceive, use, understand, and manage emotions; Yale University's Emotional

Intelligence RULER program: Recognize, Understand, Label, Express and Regulate; the Multi-Health Systems model of emotional and social skills that influence the way we perceive and express ourselves in social relationships; and Goleman, Boyatzis, and Korn Ferry's model for understanding and managing ourselves and others, to name a few.

NAME™ strikes at the heart of a stripped-down question we all face, consciously or not: What next? What do we do with our emotions when we feel them: let them out, hold them in, let them go? What do you do?

NEURO TIP

UNDERSTANDING THE RIGHT ANSWER DEFINES EMOTIONAL AWARENESS. UNDERSTANDING AND APPLYING THE RIGHT ANSWER AT THE RIGHT TIME DEFINES EMOTIONAL BRILLIANCE™.

The three general principles to accomplish Emotional Brilliance are ones you are likely already familiar with, and probably use every minute even if you don't realize it.

The first is to play to your strengths. To use an analogy, let's say you're out for dinner with a friend at a fancy Italian restaurant. She's a foodie who just got back from Florence where she fulfilled a lifelong dream of completing a three-month cooking course at the world famous Scuola di Arte Culinaria Cordon Bleu. You, on the other hand, rank macaroni and cheese as the all-time best Italian dish ever. It'd probably be a good idea to let your friend help you order since fancy Italian food is Greek to you. However, to carry this analogy further, mac and cheese would be one of your core competencies when you go to a Denny's.

By applying NAME™, you can more effectively and efficiently identify your emotional core competencies in a variety of different situations, and all in the

CHAPTER FIVE | 77

present moment. Sure, areas that you would benefit from shoring up are important to pay attention to, but not at the expense of handicapping your already-present strengths.

In fact, our research shows that excelling at just four or five of the eighteen competencies as defined by the Emotional Competence Inventory 2.0 (ECI) can lead you to greater rewards. This speaks to competency companions depending on the situation based on other research by John Zenger and Joseph Folkman as described in their book *The Extraordinary Leader*.

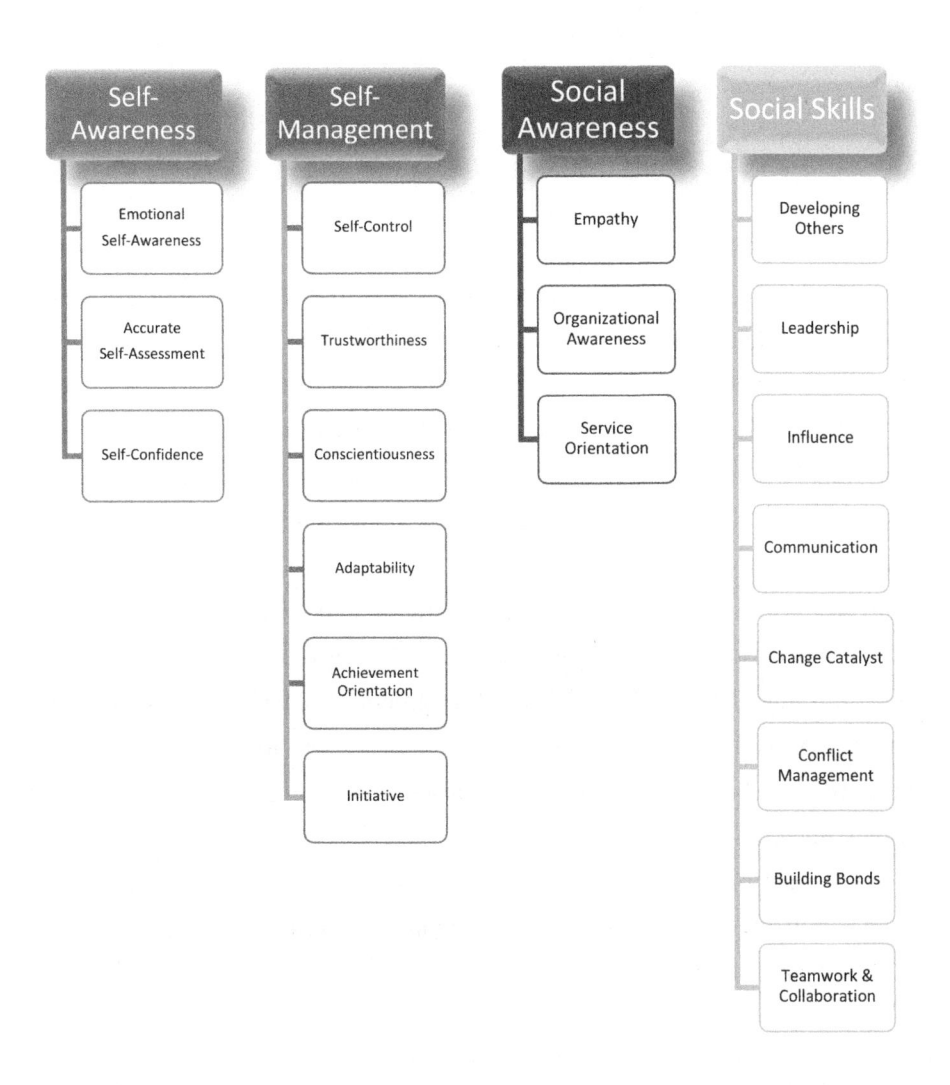

Self-Awareness	Self-Management	Social Awareness	Social Skills
Emotional Self-Awareness	Self-Control	Empathy	Developing Others
Accurate Self-Assessment	Trustworthiness	Organizational Awareness	Leadership
Self-Confidence	Conscientiousness	Service Orientation	Influence
	Adaptability		Communication
	Achievement Orientation		Change Catalyst
	Initiative		Conflict Management
			Building Bonds
			Teamwork & Collaboration

EQi 2.0 Competencies

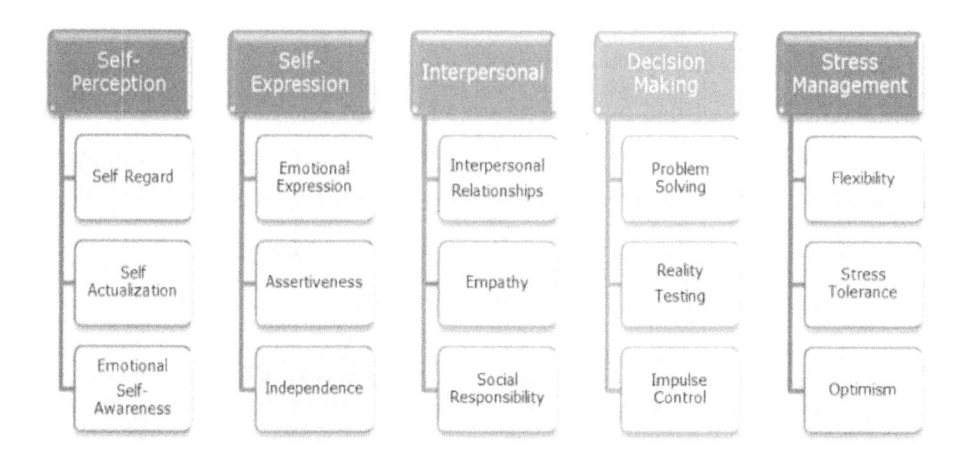

Self-Perception	Self-Expression	Interpersonal	Decision Making	Stress Management
Self Regard	Emotional Expression	Interpersonal Relationships	Problem Solving	Flexibility
Self Actualization	Assertiveness	Empathy	Reality Testing	Stress Tolerance
Emotional Self-Awareness	Independence	Social Responsibility	Impulse Control	Optimism

For example, increasing your self-confidence, trustworthiness, adaptability, empathy, and influence can position you for the best results based on your awareness of your core competencies.

The second principle that you also likely already know and apply to your emotional wellbeing is: A problem ignored is a problem that grows, or as Father Mannion says, a feeling not transformed is a feeling transmitted. Unresolved feelings may not show up in ways you'll recognize, however they are there in your sleepless nights, pints of ice cream, and high credit card debts.

They can also be in the unsatisfying parts of your relationships, overachieving and underachieving, and lapses of judgment. Yes, feelings are natural but they're not biodegradable, meaning we each need ways to keep our emotional ecology clean because it's not ashes to ashes, dust to dust, but rather ashes to ashier, dust to dustier.

As an example, one of Relly's clients, a manager named Jim who worked at a high tech firm, had been reported to human resources for being disrespectful and arrogant toward women.

He was often angry or depressed. Underneath those surface-feelings, though, hid an experience that was at the root of his deeper feelings. Jim had been married for four years in what he thought was a good relationship, until one day he came home and found his wife in bed with another man.

He left that night, never to see her again. He felt rejected, enraged, grief-stricken, hurt, embarrassed, helpless, and horrified just as anyone would, except he buried his feelings rather than deal with them. In the subsequent years, the contamination from this repression exhibited itself through his mistreatment of other women, and of himself, by becoming addicted to cocaine and alcohol.

When talking about his ex-wife, now twelve years later, his deeper feelings of grief, rage, loathing, hurt, and rejection are as present as if the shock had happened only yesterday. Twelve years later, it still impacted his trust of women, his friendships, and his unsteady risk-taking at work. Jim had what those in human resources call "rough edges." It's a term for someone they think needs coaching.

Jim's behavior was a strong indicator that his unacknowledged and avoided deeper feelings had not gone away on their own, had not biodegraded, as he had hoped. Instead, they had polluted him. By sharing his true feelings, though, he grew to feel more understood. His feelings normalized and he slowly began to accept them, and himself.

He began to realize that he wasn't horrible and worthless, but rather that he was hurt just as anyone would be in his situation, and that he could be understood, accepted, and loved by others. As a result, he began to integrate his feelings more, which led him to share them more with nurturing people and to start moving forward again.

There are a lot of people like Jim who also mistakenly think out of sight, out of mind works with their emotions. Going back to the analogy with biodegradable matter, an apple core left outdoors can take two months to degrade. While a plastic bag can take ten to twenty years, and an aluminum can eighty to two hundred years; that's a lot of environmental pollution.

Our feelings are more like an aluminum can than an apple. Unresolved feelings accrue on top of the earlier piles of unresolved feelings that rust, chip, and splinter to pollute your emotional ecosystem. That toxicity reveals itself through impatience, sarcasm, and bitterness, or in more severe cases where a post-traumatic stress disorder is present, through self-destructive behavior, reclusiveness, and insomnia.

This is particularly tricky for men who have grown up in cultures that say having emotions and feelings is effeminate. The *Harvard Business Review* published a related 2018 article titled "How Masculinity Contests Undermine Organizations" with results from a survey of thousands of workers in North America. It reveals four standards associated with a perceived masculine expression of emotions in the workplace:

1. Show no weakness
2. Possess strength and stamina
3. Put work first
4. Compete dog eat dog

The study also finds that organizations that score high on contests of masculinity tend to have more toxic leaders, less psychological safety, less employee family support, higher rates of illness and depression, and higher rates of burnout and turnover. As with many things in a capitalistic society, money talks, and what money is saying here is more emotional awareness brings more profits. Raising emotional awareness to a level of Emotional Brilliance™ brings an even higher ROI.

As we recover from the 2020 pandemic, many of our family members, friends and coworkers are likely to need a similar heightened degree of emotional awareness. It is anticipated that the associated psychological trauma will remain long after the physical health crisis ends, and that our personal interactions may very well mimic the virus in the sense that emotional distress will be triggered more often in our hyperreactive states. The real danger is when high reactivity becomes the norm.

NEURO TIP

A REACTIVE STATE CAN BECOME A REACTIVE TRAIT

To recap, the first two principles for achieving Emotional Brilliance™ are to play to your strengths and to understand that a problem ignored is a problem that grows. The third and final principle is to develop empathy. Doctors Ekman and Goleman describe this as feeling others' pain in your heart. This can then mature into "compassionate empathy" where you become more adept at being empathic without jeopardizing your own well-being, yet are still moved to take action that will alleviate others' pain. In the Greek language, this is sometimes called *agape*. Agape is love in action, much like what first responder healthcare professionals, police officers, and firefighters demonstrate.

Agape or compassion do not happen spontaneously. Rather, they arise through experience, development, and reasoning, but with practice they can become an ordinary everyday expression for a lifetime. By applying the NAME™ process, you can more easily experience agape in your own life, and with that, gain new understanding of what's most important to you and help others do the same in their lives. This circle of emotional ecology achieved and sustained through Emotional Brilliance™ mirrors our intrinsic desire to live in a community, to be a part of something bigger than ourselves.

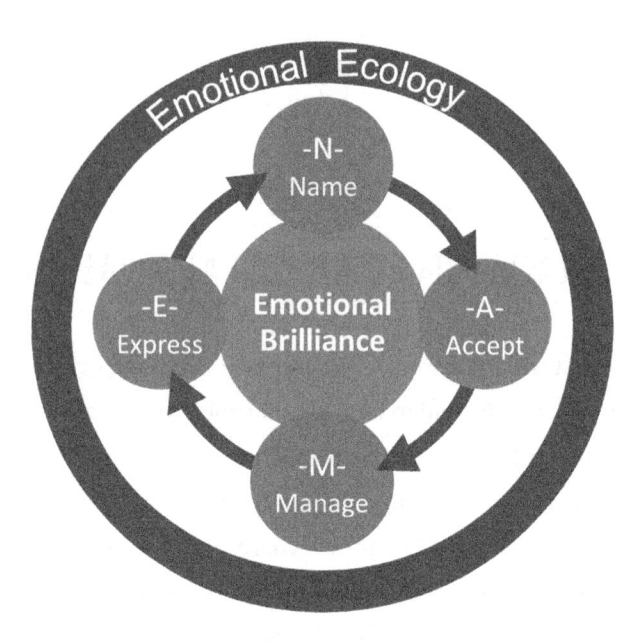

NOTICE AND NAME

"What shall I call thee? I happy am, Joy is my name."

—William Blake

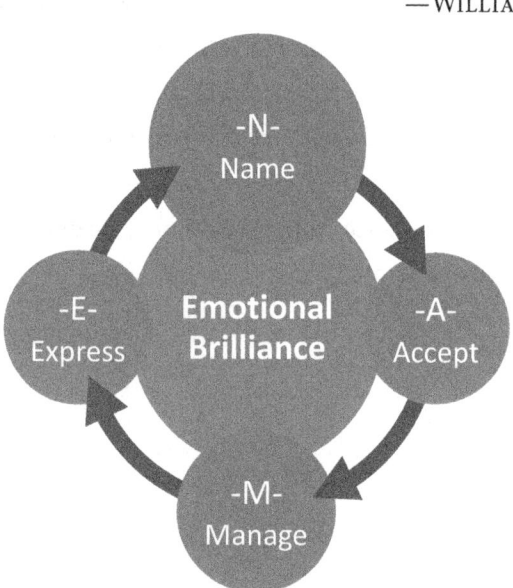

CHAPTER FIVE | 83

"Call him Voldemort, Harry," Dumbledore says. "Always use the proper name for things. Fear of a name increases fear of the thing itself." That's good advice for the young Gryffindor in J.K. Rowling's classic *Harry Potter and the Sorcerer's Stone.*

It turns out that Dumbledore's advice is good for all us, Gryffindors, Hufflepuffs and the rest. By naming your focal points, distractions, and things in between, you give yourself more power to achieve that which you are striving for. For instance, a well-known technique in personal motivation is to name your goals. As an example, "to make two new friends in the next twelve months." Along with that, to name the obstacles in your way. "I work a lot, and I'm too tired to go out."

By naming your goals and obstacles, you can track your progress, and more importantly, hold yourself accountable for what is in your control and accept that which is not. This gives better results than just keeping in mind that one day you'll go back to volunteering at the youth center or back to your Wednesday girls' night out or poker game with the guys.

The same is true with your emotional life. By naming your emotions, your prospects for greater awareness increase, which leads us to identifying and naming your emotions and feelings as the first step in the NAME™ model.

Using Plutchik's work as a guide, you feel any one of these following eight emotions, and often a number of them at the same time: joy, sadness, anger, fear, trust, disgust, surprise, and anticipation.

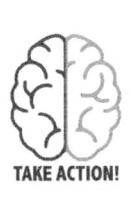

TAKE ACTION!

Think about the feelings you are having right now. It may help to close your eyes. What are you sensing in your body? Do you have a new set of feelings being created as a result of your focus, such as frustration or satisfaction?

Visit www.eblifebook.com for more details.

Let's take trust for a further example. Say you get a call from a Robert at Lucky Diamond Resorts telling you that you've won an all-expenses paid vacation, and all you have to do is give your credit card number as a show of good faith. He promises he won't charge anything on it, but still Robert says he'd feel better having something on file, with the implication you're not to be trusted.

Possibly, depending on how your day is going, you might feel angry that this guy is trying to scam you. Or surprise that this guy thinks anyone would fall for such a scheme. Or sad that this guy believes life on the fringes is the best he can do for himself. Whichever emotional reaction you have, nine out of ten of you will end it by hanging up, not bothering to try to understand how you feel in that moment.

But this nothing of an event for the nine out of ten of you is a significant event for one out of ten, or twenty-five million Americans, according to research conducted in 2018 which estimates $9.5 billion was lost to telemarketing fraud that year alone. The Federal Trade Commission further reports that in 2019, those in their twenties reported losing money in a fake check scheme twice as often as those over thirty years of age, which helps debunk the common perception that the elderly are these crooks' primary targets. Sure, we all experience Plutchik's eight universal emotions, but in this case, from a distance, it's easy to see that those twenty-five million Americans got lost in their anticipation and trust.

As another example with trust, say there's someone you only hear from when they need something. It could be a coworker, neighbor, or relative who can't seem to keep a job, but they're also someone you care about, so it's hard to tell them no. So whenever they text, email, or call, you have a wide range of conflicting feelings covering not wanting to turn your back on them while also not trusting them to stop dragging you down.

TAKE ACTION!

Think of someone or something you have mixed feelings about. Name each of those feelings even if they don't seem to make sense to you.

Visit www.eblifebook.com for more details.

The fact is, we all get lost in our feelings from time to time, no matter how smart we are. The emotional processing of minutiae in your life, like a telemarketer calling you, is remarkably similar to the emotional processing of your most important personal relationships, business dealings, and political and cultural events. By strategically applying this first step of identifying and naming your feelings as they occur, you can better direct yourself to both get closer to those you care about and protect yourself from those who don't care about you.

The Mood Meter is a good tool to help you name your feelings. It is below and also can be found free at www.moodmeterapp.com.

TAKE ACTION!

Look at the Mood Meter's four quadrants and companion list below, and name the feelings you have most of the time.

Visit www.eblifebook.com for more details.

86 | EMOTIONAL BRILLIANCE™

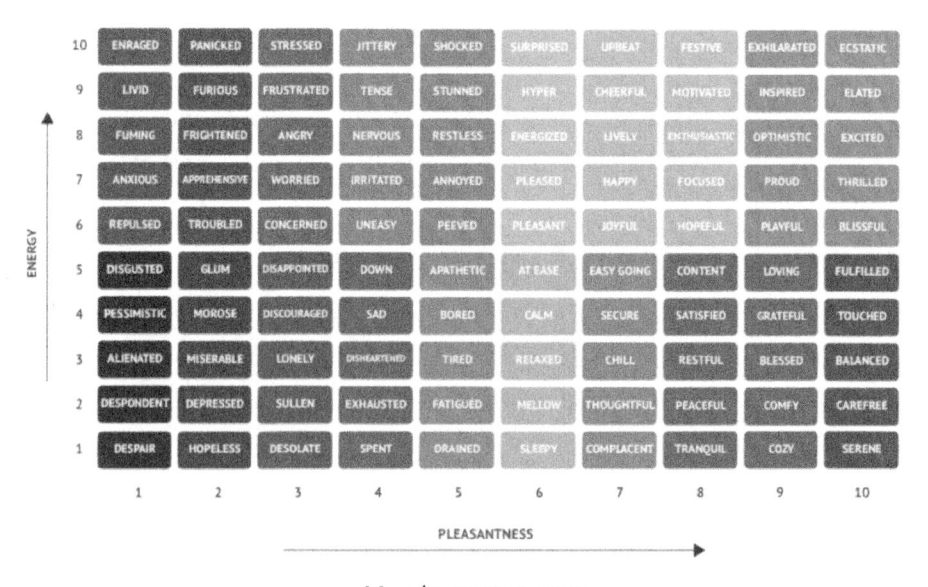

FEELINGS

10	ENRAGED	PANICKED	STRESSED	JITTERY	SHOCKED	SURPRISED	UPBEAT	FESTIVE	EXHILARATED	ECSTATIC
9	LIVID	FURIOUS	FRUSTRATED	TENSE	STUNNED	HYPER	CHEERFUL	MOTIVATED	INSPIRED	ELATED
8	FUMING	FRIGHTENED	ANGRY	NERVOUS	RESTLESS	ENERGIZED	LIVELY	ENTHUSIASTIC	OPTIMISTIC	EXCITED
7	ANXIOUS	APPREHENSIVE	WORRIED	IRRITATED	ANNOYED	PLEASED	HAPPY	FOCUSED	PROUD	THRILLED
6	REPULSED	TROUBLED	CONCERNED	UNEASY	PEEVED	PLEASANT	JOYFUL	HOPEFUL	PLAYFUL	BLISSFUL
5	DISGUSTED	GLUM	DISAPPOINTED	DOWN	APATHETIC	AT EASE	EASY GOING	CONTENT	LOVING	FULFILLED
4	PESSIMISTIC	MOROSE	DISCOURAGED	SAD	BORED	CALM	SECURE	SATISFIED	GRATEFUL	TOUCHED
3	ALIENATED	MISERABLE	LONELY	DISHEARTENED	TIRED	RELAXED	CHILL	RESTFUL	BLESSED	BALANCED
2	DESPONDENT	DEPRESSED	SULLEN	EXHAUSTED	FATIGUED	MELLOW	THOUGHTFUL	PEACEFUL	COMFY	CAREFREE
1	DESPAIR	HOPELESS	DESOLATE	SPENT	DRAINED	SLEEPY	COMPLACENT	TRANQUIL	COZY	SERENE
	1	2	3	4	5	6	7	8	9	10

PLEASANTNESS

Moodmeterapp.com

The biology behind naming emotions is also interesting. Using functional MRI, Mathew Lieberman at UCLA's Social Cognitive Neuroscience Laboratory experimented with first showing pictures of people to a test group. He reported that in response, the part of the brain known as the amygdala was activated.

Next, he asked the test group to identify the gender of each of the people in the pictures; a question that doesn't take much thinking to figure out. He reported that their answers did not produce any further activation in the amygdala.

Finally, he asked the test group what emotions they thought the people in the pictures were feeling; a question that does require a good amount of executive functioning in the prefrontal cortex part of the brain. He reports that the prefrontal cortex was activated and the amygdala was deactivated.

His conclusion is there is an inverse relationship between the prefrontal cortex and the amygdala, meaning when one is activated, the other is not. This also means that being thoughtful creates a calmer life.

By noticing and naming your own feelings, you activate your prefrontal cortex's executive functioning and put yourself one step closer to Emotional Brilliance™. Part of this process is being aware of the characteristics of your emotional life. For example, if you're in a conversation with someone and have a headache, nervous stomach, cracking voice, sweaty palms, dizziness, or shallow breath, those physical indicators can tell you a lot about your emotional state in the moment and ultimately lead you to better expressing yourself in the moment.

With the recent rise in video conferencing, a whole new set of emotionally centered physical indicators has arisen. In our in-person relationships, the brain instinctively and automatically engages in reading the facial expressions of one another. When we are in virtual conversations, the same instinct and automation kicks in; however, because of pixilation, lighting, lenses, and buffering, the brain has to work so much harder to get a reading on facial expressions.

As Kate Murphy, author of *You're Not Listening: What You're Missing and Why It Matters*, writes in *The New York Times*:

> Not only does this mess with our perception, but it also plays havoc with our ability to mirror. Without realizing it, all of us engage in facial mimicry whenever we encounter another person. It's a constant, almost synchronous, interplay. To recognize emotion, we have to actually embody it, which makes mirroring essential to empathy and connection. When we can't do it seamlessly, as happens during a video chat, we feel unsettled because it's hard to read people's reactions and, thus, predict what they will do.

Even with in-person interactions, your own defenses and those of others can make for a difficult reading of true emotional states. People who are always laughing or smiling in public might tell you in private, if they could, that they'd be crying if they weren't laughing. Others project, intellectualize, blame, charm, clown, bully, and perfect, to name a few decoys, to protect their more sensitive and vulnerable emotions. These façades are hard to keep up over time, but for many, they are worth the cost in order to feel safe, even though this kind of safety is just more self-deception. Real safety comes from being honest with ourselves.

TAKE ACTION!

Name your defenses that you fall back on the most, such as rationalizing, blaming, clowning around, and being a perfectionist.

Visit www.eblifebook.com for more details.

In addition to nonverbal cues, the verbal communications or metaphors you use can literally announce how you are feeling. For example, "My heart is racing"; "I've got this"; "Same old, same old." The things we say without thinking about them can describe our deeper feelings that otherwise seem inaccessible, ones that often originated early in life, perhaps even pre-verbally as an infant.

Emotional styles also are often established early in life, if not already an innate part of an individual's unique personality. Richard Davidson and Sharon Begley describe in *The Emotional Life of Your Brain* how we each have our own unique emotional style composed of these dimensions: Resilience, Outlook, Social Intuition, Self-Awareness, Sensitivity to Context, and Attention. The authors write that all of us fall somewhere along a continuum for each dimension; some at the extreme ends and some more in the middle. The combination of your cumulative scores along these continuums determines your emotional style.

You can apply these style guidelines to help you better understand your own emotional makeup, and from there, for example, use that knowledge to help you identify your normal range of emotional intensity. Thus, with all other factors being equal, a specific incident may trigger one person to experience it with mild frustration, while another person may experience it as enraging. This approach is compatible with Plutchik's Wheel of Emotions which diagrams a continuum of emotions passing from mild to strong, such as from apprehension to fear to terror, or from serenity to joy to ecstasy. An awareness of your emotional style can help you zero in on noticing and naming your feelings.

Rate yourself on the following traits to see if there are patterns in how you feel.

TAKE ACTION!

Resilient
Optimistic
Aware
Sensitive
Attentive

○ Not at all
○ A little
○ Somewhat
○ A lot
○ To a great extent

Visit www.eblifebook.com for more details.

ACCEPT

"Whatever you happen to be feeling at any moment is fine."

—Jim Morrison

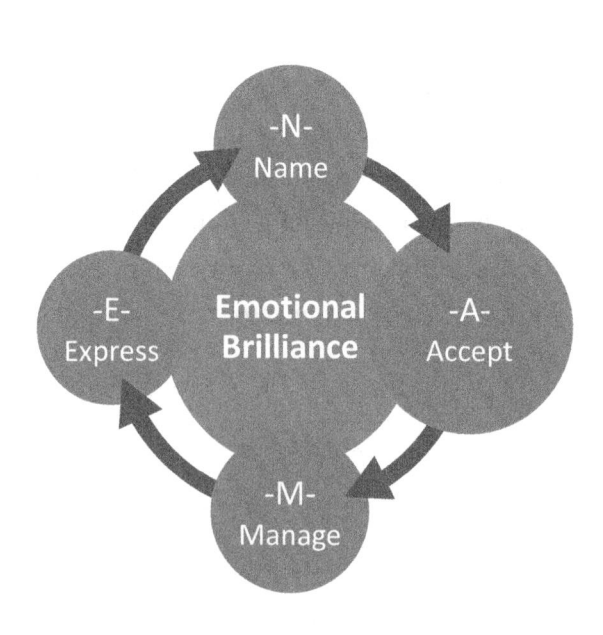

-N- Name
-A- Accept
-M- Manage
-E- Express

Emotional Brilliance

Acceptance is hardly a new concept. After all, it's applied in almost every aspect of life. For example, the famous Serenity Prayer "to accept the things I cannot change, courage to change the things I can, and wisdom to know the difference" is taped to refrigerator doors all across the country, and is a standard piece of recovery programs. However, in the world of emotions, acceptance has not caught on, and in fact is often met with counter ideas, such as there are good emotions and bad ones, positive and negative ones, life affirming and life denying ones.

Yet, in the parlance of egalitarianism, they are all equal but different.

This is not some philosophical mumbo jumbo, it's a practical part of personal integrity. Let's explain. How can any of us give into biases about emotions, many of which are just social constructs we knowingly go along with, and still claim our integrity? For example, when anyone of us says "get over it" in immediate response to sadness; "let 'em have it" in response to anger; "dial it up" in response to joy; "get a grip" in response to fear; "too cool" in response to trust; "quit being a victim" in response to disgust; "grow up" in response to surprise; or "don't set yourself up" in response to anticipation, it is almost always prematurely judgmental. In this second step of the NAME™ process—the acceptance stage—judgment has no place.

Instead, being an emotional agnostic without prejudice or favor to any emotion over another offers the clearest path. Think of it this way, skipping the acceptance of your emotions clouds your reasoning for when your judgments are appropriate. Furthermore, your principles and your integrity require you to be the biggest person you are capable of. Using Plutchik's diagram of the Wheel of Emotions, our universal eight different emotions are paired equally and oppositely: joy versus sadness; anger versus fear; trust versus disgust; and surprise versus anticipation. They mirror one another. They are vital to one another.

Mary Oliver, one of the most celebrated poets of our lifetime, expresses this in *The Uses of Sorrow*:

(In my sleep I dreamed this poem)

*Someone I loved once gave me
a box full of darkness.*

*It took me years to understand
that this, too, was a gift.*

Poets can help us learn these secrets of the heart and mind, but with some insight, we can learn this on our own, too. So if there is ever a case to be made for being open, let it involve developing your own emotional repertoire so that you have the courage to feel your disgust, to feel your anticipation, to feel all of your emotions, to be with them without censorship or guilt or politeness. To understand that all of your feelings are okay. That there are no right or wrong feelings, they are yours without judgment, and without acting on them at this acceptance stage. Yes, joy feels better, but it's not a better emotion. Fear feels worse, but it's not a lesser emotion.

This is such a vital piece to understand, because from this ground of acceptance, you can, for better or for worse, rightfully and appropriately later judge how well you manage and express your feelings.

One of the simplest ways to help condition yourself to be accepting without judgment is to adjust your view to that of an objective and curious observer. As an observer, you metaphorically take notes as you would were you a student listening with an open mind to a teacher. Some might call this being a sponge while also being aware that at a later time you will wring out the sponge, which represents in the NAME™ process the management stage.

NEURO TIP

BEING AN OBSERVER ALLOWS YOU TO GET USED TO BEING WITH YOUR FEELINGS

TAKE ACTION!

Ask yourself the following questions to help strengthen your observer-self:

a) Who do I feel comfortable expressing my feelings with?
b) What do my feelings tell me?
c) When do I feel most comfortable with my feelings?
d) Why do I best accept my feelings?
e) Visit www.eblifebook.com for more details.

Courage is often an unexpected consequence of this acceptance stage. Rather than rushing to fix ourselves or inviting others to fix us, we learn to weather the storms. We learn to tell ourselves that we will get through it and come out better for having done so. Just a reminder, observing a parade of emotions takes just as much discipline as observing a storm of them. Like them, love them, tolerate them, hate them—the same rules for acceptance apply.

TAKE ACTION!

Stop and smell the roses, slow down and let your feelings evolve at their own pace.

Visit www.eblifebook.com for more details.

Another tool to help with emotional acceptance is called "embrace the suck." It's a military term that became well-known on battlefields throughout the Gulf War. Living in the constant filth, sand, insects, scorching and freezing temperatures, with unending deployments while fitted in heavy gear trying to keep death away, and fewer and fewer breaks between missions, plus no alcohol allowed, American soldiers learned to lean into it all instead of resisting it. Staying with the discomfort had a way of diffusing it.

Far from war zones, Buddhism teaches a similar lesson from a far different approach, through an understanding of the impermanence of our existence, including that suffering will also pass. This insight opens room for your brain and body to adjust to discomfort, and thus relax resistance, generate comfort, and increase self-compassion. And so goes the saying, "We must taste the bitter before we can appreciate the sweet."

NEURO TIP

THE BETTER YOU ARE AT BEING COMPASSIONATE WITH YOURSELF, THE BETTER YOU ARE AT BEING COMPASSIONATE WITH OTHERS

TAKE ACTION!

Unplug for several hours one day a week to let yourself be with your feelings. You can sink into them better with distractions put away.

Visit www.eblifebook.com for more details.

CHAPTER FIVE | 95

This level of acceptance is not easy to attain. In fact, sometimes hitting a wall is a good reminder of this, and also that self-acceptance is the way over walls. Just ask Dana.

Dana Ackley, executive coach and leadership consultant

> I'm always building out mental models about how people work and how I work. But I think that probably the most helpful experience I had was a crisis, which is often true for folks. I have a PhD in clinical psychology and had been a clinician for about twenty-five years. I was insurance dependent. I was very successful. I had a waiting list of people. I thought at that age in my young forties I had life all figured out.
>
> Then managed care came along and told me that I was just dead wrong. I was anxious, fearful, and depressed for about a year. So I engaged in self-reflection to figure things out. What am I feeling? What are the kinds of things that drag my feelings? What are the things that are likely to trip me up and trigger the wrong response? And, despite not being perfect, despite not being all-knowing, how can I have the confidence to move forward?
>
> As I was getting more educated about how stress impacted me, I realized that sometimes before I recognized my self-talk, my lower back would tighten up. So what are my impulses telling me? If I have an impulse to run away or to lash out, that may suggest that I'm feeling kind of anxious or angry. It's an early warning device that can stop you from saying or doing an unfortunate thing, right?
>
> I don't like feeling helpless very much. Yet there are situations within which we are all helpless in some ways. I may want certain things to not be true. Maybe I don't want outside forces to disrupt

me. I figured out how to be successful, and because I don't like to feel helpless, I kept repackaging the same ways of being successful rather than adapting to the times.

If I don't adapt to the changing circumstances in which I find myself and allow myself to feel that initial sense of helplessness, perhaps despair, fear, anxiety, to just be aware, wow, these are good emotions in the sense that they warn me that something is amuck. If I allow myself to notice those feelings, I can do something about them. If I hide from my helpless feelings, then I have a problem.

What I also learned from that was resilience. It doesn't all go perfectly. There are contracts that I don't get. There are relationships that end before I wish they would. There are recessions that get in the way, and that sort of thing. I didn't know what the path through might be at that time, but I believed that there was one.

I also learned a trick to help me manage my anxiety. After I have done all I can, I tell myself I've done what I can do and need to move forward. Realizing I have alternatives has been a lifelong process.

---

1. What stands out for you in Dana Ackley's story?
2. When you're feeling down, you like to _____.

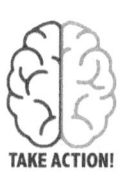

TAKE ACTION!

Practice breathing exercises to help keep yourself calm and kind when feeling upset with yourself or others. One popular exercise is "box breathing." Slowly breathe in for a count of four, hold it for a count of four, then slowly exhale for a count of four.

Visit www.eblifebook.com for more details.

MANAGE

"Don't fake it 'til you make it. Learn it as you become it."

—Keisha A. Rivers

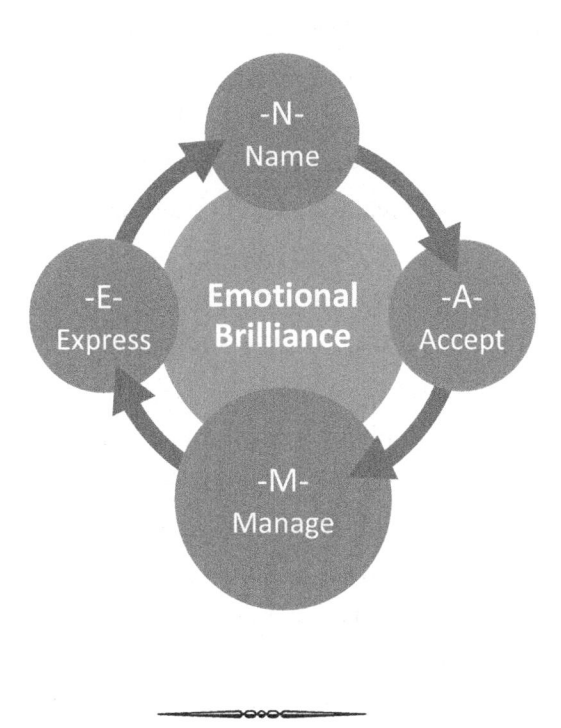

```
         -N-
        Name

-E-    Emotional    -A-
Express Brilliance  Accept

         -M-
        Manage
```

Steven Stein, CEO of Multi-Health Systems

I've been giving presentations and speeches for the last thirty or whatever years. I can speak to crowds of a thousand people. I've been on national TV shows. I don't get nervous at all when I do those. I'm excited and I'm confident. I'm also a musician. I play the saxophone. I play in a saxophone quartet and I've played in a couple of bands. But I get petrified when I have to play music in front of a crowd sometimes. It puzzles me.

Why is it—my musician friends just laugh at me because I can give a speech in front of hundreds of people and be really calm and cool—when I play a piece in front of five people and one of them might be my coach, I'm terrified? I make mistakes, it's not perfect.

I've been trying to understand this. What is it about performing music that makes me anxious and I can't overcome as easily as giving a speech in public? The answer really drove it home for me that I need to try to embrace more of the things that calm me down because I'm very much more critical when it comes to music.

I know when I'm giving a talk, if I make a mistake, I can make a joke about it or can repeat what I meant. But when it comes to music and I make a mistake, I'm done. I'm toast. If you know music and you're listening to me, you know I blew it, right? I can't go back and redo that.

So that kind of thinking is what's important. It's an important link for me to be I'm excited about playing in front of you, and I don't worry, I don't think about making mistakes. It's not even on the radar, right? So, I have to teach myself not to worry about mistakes, or if I make a mistake just keep going, it doesn't matter. It's not the end of the world.

As a musician, if you are so worried about how you're playing and making mistakes, you can't connect with the audience, you can't connect with the other band members.

Most of us get by every day and things aren't that bad, usually because we've been taught all this stuff in other areas. For example, in sports like tennis where tennis players prepare themselves before a match, what they tell themselves is really important in terms of optimum performance. In the recent US Open, for example, a nineteen-year-old female named Bianca Andreescu won. She beat Serena Williams in the finals. It was an exciting match to see how she overtook a veteran, one of the world's best tennis players.

Bianca won the first set. She was winning the second set, but then Serena started coming back. Serena is known for that. She's a tough competitor and she's known for coming back from behind. After the match, I interviewed her coach. I asked him: "What were you thinking when she started falling behind? She's nineteen years old, the crowd was so loud—you could see at one point she covered her ears."

He answered, "You know what? I was happy."

I said, "What do you mean you were happy?"

"Because we rehearsed that so many times."

This is that whole visualization thing. For a lot of people, it is not a spur-of-the-moment brilliance. For some it is, but in her case, she had practiced a hundred times in her mind playing against Serena, and Bianca's main thing was to break her serve, which she did. Her next main thing was to serve to Serena's high left side because she knew she had more trouble high left. These things were all chosen. Bianca had seen them in her mind a hundred times already. She knew exactly what to do. She knew to hit her high left and beat her on the serves.

Sometimes we look emotionally brilliant as if we did it in the spur of the moment. In high-pressure situations, it's a rare person who can, on the spur of the moment, hit the right emotion at the right time. It happens, but it's rare.

In most situations, we've learned how to put it in our repertoire and when to pull it out. The basics of running an organization call for recognizing a situation, assessing the available information, coming up with a plan, and implementing the plan. That's about the same process for the basics of running your emotional awareness: name your emotion, accept it, manage it, and then express it.

---

1. What stands out for you in Steven Stein's story?
2. What does your inner critic tell you?

This third step in the NAME™ process, managing your feelings, speaks to the tools you have in your toolbox and how versatile you are at adapting them and pivoting between them as needed. The plan is to have a toolbox that helps keep you current; meaning, it helps you manage more of your feelings in the present and reduce your backlog of unresolved feelings waiting for you to still get to them.

As an example, if you're feeling really frustrated tucked away at your home or office, you probably already know that it will help to take deep breaths, slow yourself down, and then start again with your normal relaxed breathing. That's a great tool. But not so great if you're feeling nervous up on a stage speaking to a roomful of people. In this case, a better tool would be to discreetly jot down some helpful words or positive affirmations in the margins of your speech, such as: "Breathe." "Slow." "Relax." That's a great tool, well, unless you're arguing with your spouse or loved one when you won't have a speech to read from. In this case, taking a time-out, clearing your head and then coming back and talking it out would be a better tool.

Simply taking a quick break for a sip of water, a cup of coffee or tea and focusing on the liquid as it touches your lips, floats over your tongue, melts on your taste buds, flows into your throat and down to your tummy can help you quiet yourself. Just taking a pause to look inside yourself and manage what comes next, instead of continuing to escalate or make your point is a healthy way to get in touch with yourself whenever your body starts to feel a rush. Jeff Moosa understands this.

When my wife Parveen died, I stopped everything. The clock stopped. I was married for thirty years plus. I've been working all my life sixteen to eighteen hours a day. For six months, I completely stopped.

CHAPTER FIVE | 101

I came to this country from Pakistan in 1981, coincidentally on the Fourth of July, with my wife and my son who was only twenty months old then. I did a lot of jobs in the beginning. I worked as a cashier and at a carwash, but this is such a great country. This country gives you all of the opportunities. If you are honest, work hard, and are a good entrepreneur, you can succeed.

In 1982, I got a job at Security Pacific Bank in California. It was a good experience. In 1987, I left there and we went to a small town in California. God bless my wife, I lost her in 2016, but at that time she was with me and we went and bought a small liquor store on a major street. We worked day and night. We both were still working as bankers and running our business so it was a challenge and we struggled a lot. Then we sold that business and bought another one. We started with very little capital and had very small salaries, but we always had a dream to have our own business.

My mom came from a business family, and she always said if you start something and work very hard, if you work honestly, then the sky is the limit. I thank Mom for that advice. So we took her advice and worked. In 1996 or 1997, we moved to Texas to a small town outside of Houston and bought a nice convenience store, a Texaco gasoline brand with a restaurant.

Our journey kept moving forward. In 2007, we moved to Dallas and bought a gas station with my son and daughter-in-law and found this one franchise, Church's Chicken, and we put it in the gas station.

We kept growing. We kept it moving. I had the opportunity to save some money, and I always had a dream to think big, which I still have today, so I bought a gas station jobbership. This was in 2007. A jobbership supplies different brands to different people. We started with sixty-four accounts that we supplied fuel to. I had two very nice partners with me. We called it Community Fuel of Texas, and we worked very hard.

Then we bought jobberships for three or four big fuel companies from Waco, Texas. We bought a lot more jobberships from different people so we became very big. By 2011, we were the second-largest fuel distributor in Dallas. That was a really big achievement. That was my dream. We ended up selling the company to a very strong group in Houston and made good money.

I decided to go into the franchise business next. I was already in it some with Church's Chicken. At that point, I had five or six different locations. In 2011, I got a very big opportunity to buy thirty-seven Jack in the Box stores from their corporate office in San Diego. I achieved that blessing of God, working hard with my wife, younger brother, son, and others.

A very smart and bright person named Eric Miller was my COO. He and I had an agreement when he came in that when he was ready, I would help him get into business for himself. He had worked in corporations his whole life. So in 2015, he bought some stores from me. He has five daughters and I told him they were like my own, so I said, "How about five stores, one for each of them?" He said, "Well, my wife wants one too so make it six."

In 2015, we sold the other thirty-one stores and went for a new venture with Taco Bell. Taco Bell is such a great, great, great company to work with, and the brand is so strong. We did a really good job with our thirteen stores in the San Francisco area. We were then offered ten more in San Antonio.

But that was also a very tough time for me. In 2015, I lost my mother on March 4, and on January 26, 2016, I lost my wife. They were both close to each other. Normally, the mother-in-law is never close to the daughter-in-law, but they were very close. I used to joke with my mother, "You left us and then you took my wife also." They're in heaven enjoying it now, and I'm still here.

Sometimes it's very tough because of losses. I try to pull myself up. I think in a very deep way you need to keep your emotions in a positive way. I do a lot of meditation in the morning. I get up around four o'clock, meditate and pray, and that's what helps me. I am fortunate by the grace of God to be where I am today. I am very much thankful.

---

1. What stands out for you in Jeff Moosa's story?
2. What do you need to change about yourself? Who are you changing for?

We understand this "manage" step is not easy, but you can get better at it in less time than you think. Like most things you've faced in life, it's your ability to flex and adapt, to add a new set of tools, as you let go of old ones. In this case, that involves your Emotional Brilliance™. This is what makes an easy-to-recall model like NAME™ so helpful. Particularly since effectively applying your new tools to help manage your feelings requires an awareness of your specific situation, and of the broader context. In short, context helps us remember when, where, and who might trigger us. And since situations as well as contexts will change, so too must your tools change.

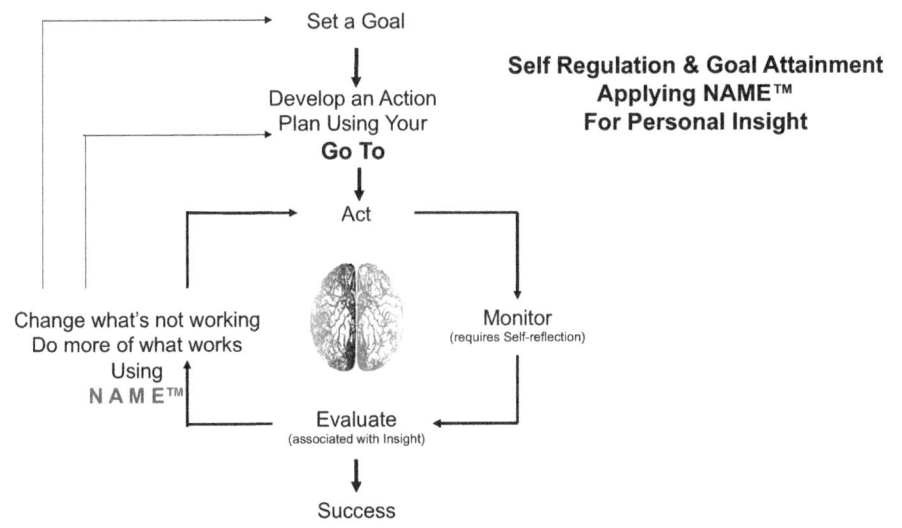

```
                    Set a Goal
                         ↓                    Self Regulation & Goal Attainment
              Develop an Action                     Applying NAME™
              Plan Using Your                      For Personal Insight
                    Go To
                         ↓
                    Act
                    
Change what's not working        Monitor
Do more of what works      (requires Self-reflection)
      Using
      N A M E™
                    Evaluate
                (associated with Insight)
                         ↓
                    Success
```

Adapted from generic model of self-regulation and goal attainment showing role of self-reflection and insight.
Anthony M. Grant, Coaching Psychology Unit, School of Psychology, University of Sydney;
John Franklin and Peter Langford, Macquarie University

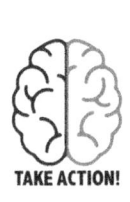

TAKE ACTION!

Remember in the beginning of the book we shared this model. We suggested you keep it handy for reference. It's important to review it, briefly use it to check in, and see what you're thinking about. Where were you when you started this journey with us, and how far have you come on your own using self-awareness and now regarding your self-regulation?

No doubt you already have some awareness about the emotional ecology in which your emotions flourish. Just by noticing the difference in yourself when things are going well as opposed to when things are falling apart is an example of you having some understanding of how broad contexts fit within your emotional ecology. Now add a situation, a public speech or a private argument, as an example, and you'll see you are working simultaneously with two different, yet merged sets of feelings—the ones you're managing contextually based on your life experience, and the ones you're managing specifically based on the situation, with each feeding the other so that the stronger you are at managing one, the stronger you are at managing the other.

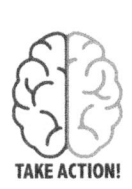

TAKE ACTION!

Movement of almost any kind is helpful for managing your feelings. It helps to change your emotional state. Walk, stretch, run, dance, cycle, hike or do another activity you enjoy.

Visit www.eblifebook.com for more details.

Please don't be fooled by people who talk about substituting this kind of management process with the fortune cookie simplicity of fake it till you make it, tell it like it is, or follow your heart, because fake people hurt themselves and others; brutal honesty isn't virtuous, it's emotionally harmful; and passion without positive clarity is followed by a hodgepodge of broken dreams.

And please don't be fooled into thinking this whole business about processing your feelings is all just analytical head stuff. Look around. There is growing evidence that the most effective managers in the private and public sectors know head stuff isn't enough, and that's why you are seeing a cultural shift toward building "emotional engagement."

Emotional engagement is a way to develop a more personal sense of ownership and to feel a part of something bigger than ourselves. For example, the sense of emotional engagement we have demonstrated by sheltering in and social distancing throughout the pandemic has made a huge difference for each of us individually and collectively. This connection we feel to one another helps comfort us as we count the loss of lives and witness the unraveling of our schools and businesses.

Consider this process a two-for-one deal in which your growing awareness of the interconnectedness between your worldview and a particular situation work in harmony to put you closer to the front door of the last step in the NAME™ process, letting your feelings out. First, though, let's look at some more strategies to help you better manage your feelings in the moment with Emotional Brilliance™.

NEURO TIP

THE BRAIN HAS A STRONG DESIRE TO STAY WITH SOMETHING ONCE IT'S BEEN LEARNED. HENCE THE SAYING "YOU CAN'T TEACH AN OLD DOG NEW TRICKS."

Dr. James Gross, one of the leading researchers of emotions, describes this management step in terms of us being able to consciously regulate the type, intensity, quality, and duration of our feelings. The following are some additional Emotional Brilliance™ tools that build on Gross's work.

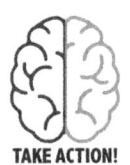

TAKE ACTION!

Take a few moments before an activity or conversation and ask yourself the questions below. This will help you better align your actions with your feelings.
- Where do I want to put my attention?
- What do I want to accomplish?
- What values do I want to bring to this situation?
- How do I bring my best self to this situation?

Visit www.eblifebook.com for more details.

TAKE ACTION!

Take a "creativity break" and let your mind wander or daydream for three minutes. This will increase your insightfulness.

Visit www.eblifebook.com for more details.

Both of these exercises also tap into an understanding of how our filters shape our emotional processes. In other words, no matter how balanced we try to be, we will always be unconsciously influenced by someone or something. Psychologist Ed Nottingham uses the writings below to emphasize the power that influences have on us:

- Shakespeare's *Hamlet*: "Nothing is either good or bad but thinking makes it so."
- Eleanor Roosevelt: "No one can make you feel anything without your consent."
- Aikido Principle: "You can't control the unexpected, but you can control your response to it."
- Henry Ford: "Whether you think you can or can't, you're right."
- William James: "Your focus becomes your experience."
- Buddha: "What we think, we become."

NEURO TIP

WE THINK OUR THOUGHTS ARE FACTS, BUT THEY ARE ONLY GUESSES

Other examples of perception errors that interfere with how well we manage our feelings include:

- all or none thinking
- disqualifying the positive
- mental filtering
- jumping to conclusions
- catastrophizing
- emotional reasoning
- "should" statements
- personalizing

Which of these thinking errors are most common for you?

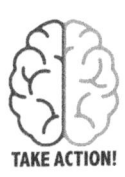

TAKE ACTION!

Set aside five to ten minutes a day to check in with yourself about how you are feeling and what you are thinking while paying attention to your breathing in that moment without judgement. This is often referred to as practicing mindfulness, and the benefits include greater compassion and empathy.

Visit www.eblifebook.com for more details.

CHAPTER FIVE | 109

EXPRESS

"Live life as though nobody is watching, and express yourself as though everyone is listening."

—NELSON MANDELA

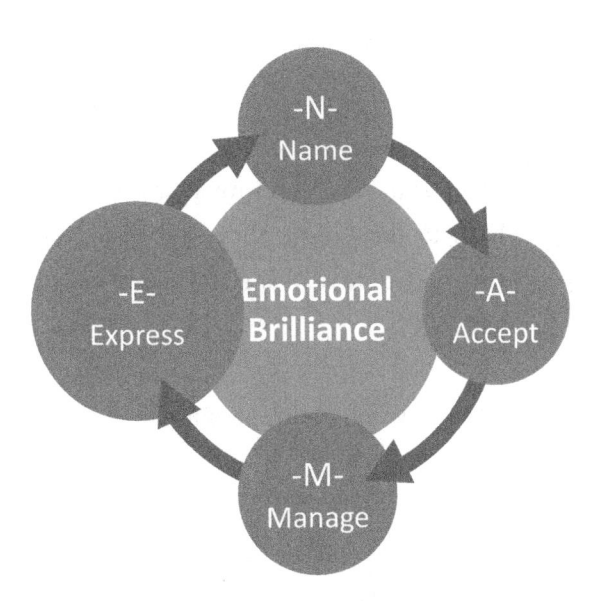

The fourth and final step in the NAME™ process is express. Insensitive things you say to others don't just hurt their feelings, they hurt their brain and your brain too. It turns out that "there are no free lunches" even applies to people in conversations, according to recent brain research showing that insensitive communications damage neural pathways in both the giver and receiver.

For example, neurologist and bestselling author Andrew Newberg and coauthor Mark Robert Waldman write in *Words Can Change Your Brain* that just five to ten minutes of ruminating can hurt your memory and impulse control. But they also offer a path forward through what they call compassionate communication. Their plan is to not only improve your communication skills, but also your brain health and that of those you communicate with. There are a number of pieces to this compassionate communication model, all of which match up nicely with our own NAME™ model. Four are particularly relevant here:

- Speak appreciatively
- Listen deeply, generously
- Speak slowly
- Speak warmly

TAKE ACTION!

Enter a conversation with a plan of talking less. Paraphrase back to them what they said to let them know you see their perspective. See if this alone increases your listening abilities.

Visit www.eblifebook.com for more details.

Even when you are at your wit's end, by the time you've gone through the first three steps of the NAME™ process—name, accept and manage—your expression of your feelings can still come out appropriately. With this new research, though, if appropriateness doesn't motivate you, then hopefully the long-term health of your neurosystem will. And if that's not reason enough when your feelings are so pent up that you can't keep the words from flying out, well, consider the likely results.

The way you express yourself directly correlates with the response from the person you are speaking with. Don't take our word for it, or that of Chris Voss, former FBI hostage negotiator and author of the runaway bestseller *Never Split the Difference: Negotiating as If Your Life Depended on It*, or Kerry Patterson, researcher on performance, behavioral drivers and lead author of the must-read *Crucial Conversations: Tools for Talking When Stakes Are High*, or Robert Cialdini, seminal researcher on the science of influence and author of the classic book *Influence: The Art and Science of Persuasion*. Try it out for yourself with this little experiment.

Let's start with a statement meant to give you comfort, and you decide if it works or not:

"You'll be okay. They say 'fail forward' so just roll with it, even though you've blown it more than anybody I've ever known or ever even heard of."

Let's try this one meant to be empathic:

"That's sad about your health insurance, but if you never got sick you wouldn't need it. So really it's up to you."

One more, this time meant to be supportive:

"Great news! Really happy for you! Now you can pay back all those people you sponged off of."

These are funny examples, but even more so they're designed to be easy to see through as a way to help you get better at seeing through your own and others' more tangled emotional expressions. This last step in the NAME™ model, expression, completes a process through which you can more often communicate how you're feeling, on-point and in the moment. Below are some strategies to help you achieve this.

NEURO TIP

WRITING HELPS THE BRAIN PROCESS FEELINGS

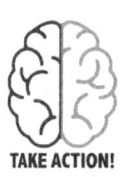

TAKE ACTION!

Keep a daily journal in which you write down how you feel. This will help you unburden yourself from pent-up feelings and also maintain your emotional ecosystem so that you increase the number of your appropriate expressions.

Visit www.eblifebook.com for more details.

TAKE ACTION!

Run an Emotional Audit on yourself when you feel upset as a way to slow your reactivity and thus reduce the number of your inappropriate expressions. Ask yourself these questions:
   a) What am I thinking?
   b) What am I feeling?
   c) What do I want now?
   d) How am I getting in my own way?
   e) What do I need to do differently now to bring forward my best self?

Visit www.eblifebook.com for more details.

CHAPTER FIVE | 113

The more you use the Emotional Audit, the more you will notice patterns in what you think and feel when triggered, along with how you get in your own way. Naming these pattern helps you be aware of them and gives you more choices and opportunities.

An example of using an emotional audit involves John, a guy known for his hot temper. He knew it himself, and his supervisor had already noted this in his personnel files.

One day, John was giving a presentation at a company sales meeting when he lost it and yelled at some of his team members to put their computers and phones away and pay attention. This worked in that they did close their devices, however it also cemented in their minds that he was nothing more than a hot-head and long overdue to be given the boot.

What happened? John felt pressured to do a good job since he had prepared the whole presentation by himself. This was by choice because he could have delegated a lot of it. Plus, earlier a few people who were supposed to attend said they couldn't because some of the company executives had wanted to play golf with them instead. The final straw was when his time reserved for the company's conference room had to be cut short to fit in another department's urgent meeting.

So John's feelings were already piled up in a mess before his presentation had even started. He went into it feeling embarrassed, disrespected, and resentful so it's really no surprise that he expressed himself poorly.

He only learned about the emotional audit tool after that meeting, but in hindsight, he went through the steps to better prepare himself for the next time he felt an outburst coming. Below are his answers.

a) What am I thinking? *What is wrong with them? I already told them.*
b) What am I feeling? *I'm so angry!*
c) What do I want now? *For them to pay attention, get off their phones and computers and support me.*

d) How am I getting in my own way? *I am fuming and ready to scream at them.*
e) What do I need to do differently to bring my best self forward? *I need to take some deep breaths, calm myself down, ignore them for now, and talk to them later when I am calmer.*

TAKE ACTION!

Write down three things every day that you are grateful for as a way to help soothe your feelings and reduce the chances of you expressing yourself inappropriately.

Visit www.eblifebook.com

CONCLUSION

Emotional Brilliance™ represents an understanding beyond the essentials of emotional awareness to provide better adaptation in an evolving world. It involves leveraging your best emotional competencies—your best emotional strengths and strategies—to take in the best perceptions from your own internal processing and from that of others, and then respond to the situation with your best self-expression, all in the present moment.

Your emotional competencies can also be thought of as your "Go To" practices and actions. They represent your feelings, values, and preparations for Emotional Brilliance™. For some, their emotional competencies have been present since early in life like Saint Mother Teresa, and then get developed further like Monsignor Michael Mannion, while for others, they discover and develop them later in life like Marshall Goldsmith or Jeff Moosa.

For example, from some of the stories throughout this book, we know that Conan Silveira makes friends with his feelings and teaches athletes to do the same. Noel Tichy asks himself every day what is it he and his students from the MBA Global Partnership at the Ross School of Management, University of Michigan can do to serve people in their communities. Dana Ackley confronts his feelings, takes appropriate action, and then lets go knowing that he has done all he can. Ramu Damodaran transforms his feelings about global injustice into action through the United Nations. George Piro empathizes even with criminals to help him solve FBI cases.

We also know that emotions influence decision-making like Debby Elnatan did with her strong intuition as a mother to find a way to help her son explore the world, and in the process, give other parents and their children a way to do the same. If you feel strong, confident, and energetic, you are more likely to make decisions based on short cuts or gut reactions, which will work well for some decisions but may not bode well for big ones. If you feel anxious, your decisions are more likely to be made with a focus on details, which will work well for balancing a budget but not so well when reconciling a broken relationship.

The NAME™ model of emotions—Name, Accept, Manage, and Express—helps you make better decisions by offering an effective and efficient way to gain a handle on your emotional life, and with practice, to gain Emotional Brilliance™.

As the world seems to be getting smaller and spinning faster, the time to embrace the natural evolutionary arc of our emotional development has never been greater. In fact, one of the gifts of Emotional Brilliance™ is that it centers on the present moment, which means the processes we have described will be as relevant tomorrow as they are today. By learning and applying it now, you set yourself on a smooth course for when the sun shines, and for a steady hand at the helm for when it doesn't.

Remember, this is a journey of discovery, of human kindness toward yourself and those you care about. Together, we can transform ourselves through less than one generation of applied emotional and social intelligence. And through every thoughtful human interaction, we become better, not more successful, but as Monsignor Michael Mannion shared, we become more significant.

As we touch the lives of others every day, we all learn to become more human just by becoming more aware. Not by science, or wealth, or mere intelligence. It's our Emotional Brilliance™ that will make the difference between winners and losers in this quickly evolving world.

CONCLUSION

"Never put a single thought of weakness in the flourishing minds of children. Fill them up with vigor and compassion, for their character will define the future of the entire human species."

—Abhijit Naskar, *The Art of Neuroscience in Everything*

CASE STUDIES

In the following pages, we share the NAME™ model in an easy-to-use NAME™ Template to assist you on your own road to discovering your Emotional Brilliance™. We've also included some real-life case studies as helpful examples for you to see how others have approached this.

Visit www.eblifebook.com for more tools, checklists, assessments, learning programs, executive coaching, and speaking for you, your team, and your organization.

Angel of Lebanon

N.A.M.E. Your Challenge	
Emotional Brilliance Template - Part I	
What is your challenge	Dr. Zeina Ghossoub is a colleague of ours in Lebanon that demonstrates Emotional Brilliance and utilizes many of the tools we speak about in the book. She has dual citizenship with the US and Lebanon. Zeina has a Ph.D. in Counseling Psychology, is an Executive Coach, a certified nutritionist, has a wellness clinic in Lebanon, is a frequent guest on TV imparting emotional intelligence advice to viewers. She is also one of the highest rated coaches in Lebanon and president of the local International Coach Federation. **Before COVID-19 hit:** • There has been an ongoing revolution since October, 2019 going on in Lebanon • There has been government inequality, corruption, sexual inequality and businesses going bankrupt • Costs went up 50%, gas up 30%, by the end of year there will be 50D% poverty • People feeling fearful, toxic, insecure, injustice and angry • Only able to take $100 dollars out of the bank at one time **Since COVI -19** • Her husband is an emergency physician in Houston unable to travel home and she is unable to travel to the US • She is very worried about her husband catching the virus and a she won't be there. • The banks are closed and no one can get their money out • They are sheltering in and she has two teenagers at home • Works 11 AM – 9 PM as an executive coach to clients along with a variety of coach related meetings • Takes care of two sets of parents
N = Notice and Name the key feelings you are having regarding this challenge	Zeina felt anxiety, worry and stress
A = Accept these feelings. What will help you to accept and befriend these feelings?	She accepts the anxiety as real and accepts this is what her life is now

N.A.M.E. Your Challenge	
Emotional Brilliance Template - Part II	
M = Manage what thoughts and actions will help you navigate this challenge. What do you summon or develop?	
"Go-to" Practice: Key values, feelings, self-statements, images, etc., to bring your best to the challenge.	Love, compassion, service, and giving back
Your Go-To Thoughts: Refer to N.A.M.E. process	• Focusing on how she can give back and help others. • Brainstorming meeting with the ICF chapter about what else they can do? • What is working with us? • Thinking of what she has gratitude for? • Changing her focus to the positive and service.
Your Go-To Actions: Refer to N.A.M.E. process	• Starts her day with exercise, prayer and reaching out to others which inspires her. • Has a NGO where she's raising money for food and delivers food to families. • As the ICF president she leads a support group for coaches. • She is on TV twice a week imparting information, support, and wisdom to the country. • With her family she has implemented a gratitude jar that her kids write in every day. • She has them doing volunteer work giving to others. Before COVID and social distancing they were visiting an orphanage.

N.A.M.E. Your Challenge	
Emotional Brilliance Template - Part III	
E = Express how will you express this feeling.	
To Yourself - journal, etc.	• Sharing her inspirational message on TV • Using Instagram for live programs • Sharing feelings with her two kids • Connecting daily with her husband • Sharing guidance and inspiration for the coaches within the local ICF chapter Zeina is truly mastering her moments for good and being very intentional about her focus and actions. In this incredible time of uncertainty and stress she's applying many of the emotional brilliance tools.

All rights reserved Greenberg & Nadler 2020
Emotional Brilliance: Living A Stress Less Fear Less Life

Tech Wiz

N.A.M.E. Your Challenge
Emotional Brilliance Template - Part I

What is your challenge	**Chief Technology Officer who is moving the company to virtual** Tom is the Chief Technology Officer, CTO, who was in the midst of a major IT conversion when his 1.2-billion-dollar financial company decided to have most employees move to work from home because of the COVID 19. 1. It was challenging that many of the processes were still pencil and paper. 2. The organization had to move 185 people off campus. 3. They had no laptops to give the employees initially. 4. The CIO purchased 65 laptops in 3 days. 5. The laptops didn't have mouses so people had to learn to use their touch pads. 6. He worked it out that the other 100 could take their desktops and monitors home. 7. He led his small IT department and customer service to calm people and the organization while in the midst of such great change. 8. He got all staff hooked-up with email and phone service. 9. Tom was only sleeping 3-4 hours a night and basically working two shifts.
N = Notice and Name the key feelings you are having regarding this challenge	Tom was able to identify that he felt stress, anxiety and guilt. The telltale sign for him was when he couldn't remember his words as fast as usual.
A = Accept these feelings. What will help you to accept and befriend these feelings?	He owned these feelings and stayed with them until he was ready to move on.

N.A.M.E. Your Challenge
Emotional Brilliance Template - Part II

M = Manage what thoughts and actions will help you navigate this challenge. What do you summon or develop?

"Go-to" Practice: Key values, feelings, self-statements, images, etc., to bring your best to the challenge.	He didn't want to let others down or disappoint them. He valued responsibility and integrity and it was motivating him.
Your Go-To Thoughts: Refer to N.A.M.E. process	• He thought about how this needs to be a Win-Win for people. • He wants to do what is best for others. • He sees this as a challenge to conquer.
Your Go-To Actions: Refer to N.A.M.E. process	• He uses a yawning exercise once an hour. • He walks to nearby lake during the day as a work break. • He started using the Take a Break Meditation App in the mornings before work. • He used the Emotional Audit questions: What am I thinking, feeling, wanting, how am I getting in my own way, and what do I need to do differently?

N.A.M.E. Your Challenge
Emotional Brilliance Template - Part III

E = Express how will you express this feeling.

To Yourself - journal, etc.	• He held daily communication meetings with his team. • He celebrated their accomplishments. • He nominated the customer service team for a big company reward. • He regularly coaches and motivates his team.

All rights reserved Greenberg & Nadler 2020
Emotional Brilliance: Living A Stress Less Fear Less Life

NAME™ TEMPLATE

Feel free to use the template as a first step. Visit www.eblifebook.com for more information to TAKE ACTION and complete your "GO TOs."

Instructions Part A.
NAME™ Your Emotional Brilliance™!

Step 1. Read all the questions in the associated NAME™ Questionnaire

Step 2. Follow how each of these questions appears in the NAME™ Template. (Consider all the questions before moving on)

Step 3. Answer each question as stated in the NAME™ Questionnaire and write your answers in the space provided.
    You may find it easier to write your answers on the NAME™ Questionnaire before you insert them into the NAME™ Template.

Step 4. Insert your answers from the NAME™ Questionnaire into the NAME™ Template.
    Take a moment to review your answers and how they flow in the NAME™ Template.
    Do you see any patterns or opportunities in the completed NAME™ Template for clues about when you may be using your "GO TO" feelings in your answers?

You may have more than one "GO TO" for daily situations in addition to those special "UNKNOWN" situations that crop up from time to time.

Your "Emotional Ecology" may affect your "GO TO" feelings. (For example: sleep, diet, exercise, work, home, familiar stress or a more demanding stress)

Instructions Part B.

For a guide to using your answers in the NAME™ Template to find your most appropriate "GO TO" feelings visit eblifebook.com.

You never know what you are truly capable of until you safely experiment with guidance to grow your capability.

We are eager to support your Emotional Brilliance™ so please visit us often for updates to continue your journey.

NAME™ YOUR CHALLENGE MODEL QUESTIONNAIRE

(Refer to NAME™ process in Chapter 5)

EMOTIONAL BRILLIANCE – PART 1

What is your challenge?

N = Notice and Name the key feelings you are having regarding this challenge.

A = Accept these feelings. What will help you to accept and befriend these feelings?

EMOTIONAL BRILLIANCE PART II

M = Manage what thoughts and actions will help you navigate this challenge. What do you summon or develop?

"GO TO" Practice: Key values, feelings, self-statements, images, etc., to bring your best to the challenge:

Your "GO TO" thoughts: Refer to NAME™ process:

Your "GO TO" actions: Refer to NAME™ process:

EMOTIONAL BRILLIANCE PART III

E = Express how you will express this feeling

To yourself—by journaling, etc:

To others: Who will be able to hear you, not fix you, but support you?

How will you ask them to listen to you? What is your soft start-up?

What kind of support do you want?

What are you going to say?

NAME™ TEMPLATE | 131

| | N.A.M.E. Your Challenge |
	Emotional Brilliance Template - Part I
What is your **challenge**	
N = Notice and **Name** the key feelings you are having regarding this challenge	
A = Accept these feelings. What will help you to accept and befriend these feelings?	

N.A.M.E. Your Challenge Emotional Brilliance Template - Part II	
M = Manage what thoughts and actions will help you navigate this challenge. What do you summon or develop?	
"Go-to" Practice: Key values, feelings, self-statements, images, etc., to bring your best to the challenge.	
Your Go-To Thoughts: Refer to N.A.M.E. process	
Your Go-To Actions: Refer to N.A.M.E. process	

N.A.M.E. Your Challenge
Emotional Brilliance Template - Part III

E = Express: How will you express this feeling?

To Yourself - journal, etc.	
To Others: Who will be able to hear you, not fix you, but support you?	
How will you ask them to listen to you? What is your soft start-up?	
What kind of support do you want?	
What are you going to say?	

All rights reserved Greenberg & Nadler 2020
Emotional Brilliance: Living A Stress Less Fear Less Life

BIBLIOGRAPHY

Anderson, Scott C, John F Cryan, and Ted Dinan. 2017. *The Psychobiotic Revolution*. Washington, D.C: National Geographic.

Brach, Tara. 2019. *Radical Compassion: Learning to Love Yourself and Your World with the Practice Of RAIN*. New York: Viking.

Brackett, Marc A. 2019. *Permission to Feel: Unlocking the Power of Emotions to Help Our Kids, Ourselves, and Our Society Thrive*. New York: Celadon Books.

Buckingham, Marcus. 2005. *The One Thing You Need to Know: . . . About Great Managing, Great Leading, and Sustained Individual Success*. New York: Free Press.

Carroll, Pete. 2020. "ADJUSTING TO DISRUPTION—Compete to Create". *Compete to Create*. https://competetocreate.net/adjusting-to-disruption/.

Cherniss, Cary, and Daniel Goleman. 2001. *The Emotionally Intelligent Workplace: How to Select for, Measure, and Improve Emotional Intelligence in Individuals, Groups, and Organizations*. 1st ed. San Francisco: Jossey-Bass.

Childre, Doc Lew, and Deborah Rozman. 2006. *Transforming Anxiety*. Oakland, Calif.: New Harbinger Publications, Inc.

Cialdini, Robert B. 2016. *Pre-Suasion: A Revolutionary Way to Influence and Persuade*. New York: Simon & Schuster.

Dalai Lama, and Paul Ekman. 2008. *Emotional Awareness: Overcoming the Obstacles to Psychological Balance and Compassion*. 1st ed. New York: Times Books.

Damasio, Antonio R. 2018. *The Strange Order of Things: Life, Feeling, and The Making of Cultures*. New York: Pantheon Books.

Ekman, Paul. 2016. "What Scientists Who Study Emotion Agree About". *Perspectives on Psychological Science* 11 (1): 31-34. doi:10.1177/1745691615596992.

Emmons, Robert A. 2016. *The Little Book of Gratitude: Create a Life of Happiness and Wellbeing by Giving Thanks.* London: Gaia.

Gervais, Michael. 2019. "How to Stop Worrying about What Other People Think of You". *Harvard Business Review.* https://hbr.org/2019/05/how-to-stop-worrying-about-what-other-people-think-of-you.

Grant, Anthony M., John Franklin, and Peter Langford. 2002. "The Self-Reflection and Insight Scale: A New Measure of Private Self-Consciousness". *Social Behavior and Personality: An International Journal* 30 (8): 821-835. doi:10.2224/sbp.2002.30.8.821.

Greenberg, Cathy. 2009. *What Happy Working Mothers Know: How New Findings In Positive Psychology Ca.* 1st ed. Hoboken, NJ: John Wiley & Sons.

Greenberg, Cathy, and TC North. 2014. *Fearless Leaders: Sharpen Your Focus: How the New Science of Mindfulness Can Help You Reclaim Your Confidence.* Cardiff-by-the-Sea: Waterside Productions.

Gross, James J. 1998. "The Emerging Field of Emotion Regulation: An Integrative Review". *Review of General Psychology* 2 (3): 271-299. doi:10.1037/1089-2680.2.3.271.

Grossman, Lt. Col. Dave and Paulsen, Kristine (2016) Assassination Generation. New York: Little, Brown and Company

Grossman, Dave, Kristine Paulsen, and Katie Miserany. 2016. *Assassination Generation: Video Games, Aggression, and the Psychology of Killing.* New York: Little, Brown and Company.

Harvard Business Review, Peter Drucker, Clayton M. Christensen, and Daniel Goleman. 2011. *HBR's 10 Must Reads on Managing Yourself.* Boston: Harvard Business Review Press.

Harvard Business Review, Daniel Goleman, Richard E Boyatzis, Annie McKee, and Sydney Finkelstein. 2015. *HBR's 10 Must Reads on Emotional Intelligence.* Boston: Harvard Business Review Press.

Hawkins, David. 2002. *Power Vs. Force: The Hidden Determinants of Human Behavior*. Carlsbad, Calif: Hay House.

Helling, Steve. 2019. "Tiger Woods 'Thinks about His Sex Scandal Every Day,' Says Source". *PEOPLE.Com*. https://people.com/sports/tiger-woods-sex-scandal-thinks-about-every-day/.

Luckner, John L, and Reldan Nadler. 1997. *Processing the Experience: Enhancing and Generalizing Learning*. Dubuque, IA: Kendall/Hunt Publishing Company.

McGonigal, Kelly. 2019. *The Joy of Movement: How Exercise Helps Us Find Happiness, Hope, Connection, and Courage*. New York: Avery Publishing Group.

Nadler, Reldan S. 2011. *Leading with Emotional Intelligence: Hands-On Strategies for Building Confident and Collaborative Star Performers*. New York: McGraw-Hill Education.

Nottingham, Ed. 2014. "Becoming an Emotionally Intelligent Leader: Attitude and Leadership". *Success and the Subconscious Mind*. http://successandthesubconsciousmind.locusmindset.com/wp-content/uploads/2019/10/Becoming-an-Emotionally-Intelligent-Leader-REVISED-3-27-17.pdf.

Peña-Sarrionandia, Ainize, Moïra Mikolajczak, and James J. Gross. 2015. "Integrating Emotion Regulation and Emotional Intelligence Traditions: A Meta-Analysis". *Frontiers in Psychology* 6. doi:10.3389/fpsyg.2015.00160.

Porges, Stephen W. 2017. *The Pocket Guide to the Polyvagal Theory*. New York: W.W. Norton.

Rosenberg, Marshall B. 2003. *Nonviolent Communication: A Language of Life: Life-Changing Tools for Healthy Relationships*. Encinitas, CA: PuddleDancer Press.

Rueven Bar-on, R. (2011) Multi-Health Systems, (2011) The Emotional-Quotient Inventory 2.0: User's handbook, Toronto, ON: Multi-Health Systems.

Stulberg, Brad, and Steve Magness. 2017. *Peak Performance: Elevate Your Game, Avoid Burnout, and Thrive with the New Science of Success*. New York: Rodale Press.

Tichy, Noel M., and Andrew R McGill. 2003. *The Ethical Challenge: How to Lead with Unyielding Integrity.* San Francisco: Jossey-Bass.

Vance, Erik. 2016. *Suggestible You: The Curious Science of Your Brain's Ability to Deceive, Transform, and Heal.* Washington DC: National Geographic Society.

Webb, Thomas L., Eleanor Miles, and Paschal Sheeran. 2012. "Dealing with Feeling: A Meta-Analysis of The Effectiveness of Strategies Derived from the Process Model of Emotion Regulation". *Psychological Bulletin* 138 (4): 775-808. doi:10.1037/a0027600.

Zenger, John H, and Joe Folkman. 2009. *Extraordinary Leader: Turning Good Managers into Great Leaders.* 2nd ed. New York: McGraw-Hill.

ACKNOWLEDGMENTS

CATHY'S:

My deepest gratitude to all of my loving families; I'm fortunate to have many: my natural born family including the mother of Olivia, my daughter Elisabeth and son-in-law, Andy; Aunt Nancy, Joanna, Elaina, and of course my brothers Phil and Fred; my amazing nieces and cousins; my outstanding collaborative family including Relly (my true north guide) and Cheryl Ebner (the creative mind); my handcrafted family in Philly, Florida, Virginia Beach, and forever V1K1; my exciting family of coaches, clients, colleagues, and academics; my fearless family of working warriors across all arms of the military and law enforcement, who I serve as "the guardian angel of pirates who hunt pirates" along with Father Mike (literally a godsend); particularly Special Operations Forces, the United States Army Special Forces, and now healthcare (congratulations to my winning team at "Operation Save a Doc": Dan Monti, Anthony Bazzan, Ken Sbat, Joseph Koen and Naim); my family of deeply meaningful friends like Johanna, Zeina, Kathy Lubbers, Allen Pathmarajah, and Andrei Arlovski from around the globe, and to all of you—you know who you are when you read this.

Gratitude for the www.eblifebook.com team at Syntax + Motion and Viki Winterton, Insights Publishing.

Special appreciation to Bill Gladstone at Waterside Productions for having me back for another run, and to the wonderful readers who give me the best feeling of hope for a more compassionate way of being

—together or apart—

Big Hugs!

RELLY'S:

I want to thank my family mentioned in the dedication, Martin S., L.O.M. and Nancy. Also for my brother Van for creative inspiration and playfulness, broth-er-in law Larry for his steadfastness, excitability, and passion.

Julie, Dillon, and Kensey for their love, support, and sensitivity, and for teaching me about emotional intelligence. Lux and Gregg for our adventures, support, and general silliness.

To my professional colleagues at the College of Executive Coaching, Consulting of Psychology Society, and emotional intelligence researchers and practitioners from whom I continue to learn.

To all my clients who taught me about best practices and all the people we interviewed for the book and through the *Leadership Development News* pod-casts. Special thanks to my VSVS team, Naim and Zeina, for their inspiration, collaboration and heartfelt friendship.

To Dr. Cathy Greenberg who has been an inspiration for Emotional Brilliance though her passion, patience, generosity, adaptability, creativity, and general always good vibes. Thank you all.

EMOTIONAL BRILLIANCE™

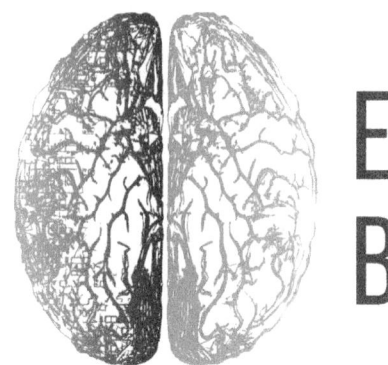

Access Bonus Tools, Tips & Resources
Valued at over $299
You need to enhance Your Emotional Brilliance™

http://eblifebook.com

*Your gift for rising above success to significance
from the authors
Dr. Cathy and Dr. Relly*

TAKE ACTION!

Made in the USA
Middletown, DE
06 April 2024